The
Final Abode
of
Consumer Society

Adnan Sarhan

Sufi Foundation of America
Torreon, NM

Published by:
Sufi Foundation of America
P.O. Box 170
Torreon, NM 87061
(505)384-5135

Cover art by Adnan Sarhan
Edited by Dr. Michelle Peticolas and Gwen Gosé

Library of Congress Catalog Card No.: 93-086350

ISBN: 1-884328-00-8

Printed and bound in the United States of America

Printed on acid-free papers

"I discard the burden of material on my shoulder as I discard the shirt off my back. Could you do that? At any time, I could put my shirt on, drive a car, or watch television, but I limit myself and I plunge into the spirit to be joyful and happy. With the spirit you never worry. Material with the spirit, you will be in heaven. And material without spirit, you are in hell." -- Adnan Sarhan

About Adnan Sarhan . . .

Sufi Master Adnan Sarhan is director of the Sufi Foundation of America and a member of five Sufi orders: Qadri, Naqshibandi, Rafai, Mevlevi, and Malamati. Internationally known for the Shattari (Rapid) Method, his work develops higher intelligence and awareness, and causes people to become creative and innovative by destroying all types of bad habits.

Adnan leads participants in a wide range of timeless techniques. Based on various traditions of scholarship, meditative sciences, physical exercise, mystical dance and music, the work signals a connection to the past which stretches back twelve hundred years. Exercises, meditation, drumming, movement, dancing and whirling are used to develop the higher intelligence of the heart, improve will power, heighten concentration, bring better personality, produce bodily changes like slower heart rates and lower blood pressure, and produce shifts in perception which result in clarity of thinking, improved memory and positive attitude.

Over the years, Adnan has conducted workshops at prestigious institutions throughout the United States and many other countries of the world including the United Nations in New York, St. James' Church in London, Alhambra Palace in Granada, Spain, the World Congress of Psychology in Switzerland, a grand concert at the Otto Zutz in Barcelona, Spain, the Earth Summit in Brazil, the Cathedral Church of St. John the Divine, New York, the Unitarian Society of Whittier, California, Esalen Institute in Big Sur, California, and conferences of Humanistic Psychology.

Last year he received a special invitation from the Russian Parliament to visit Moscow. Each summer he directs an intensive two month workshop at the Sufi Foundation Retreat Center in the Manzano Mountains of New Mexico. For further information about the summer program and Adnan's touring schedule, contact:

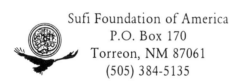

Sufi Foundation of America
P.O. Box 170
Torreon, NM 87061
(505) 384-5135

Contents

The Final Abode of Consumer Society

Consumer people consume themselves in the rage of their own selfish lust and uncompromising false desires. In doing so, they burn their spirit. When the spirit is gone, they will be gone with it, but in a different direction. It doesn't matter that they are living because their life has lost the value of life. A life without value is a sad life. It is dreary, dismal and dispirited. To live it or not live, it is equal.

Life without spirit is a sparkless life and the emptiness in the eyes reveals inner death.

A man without spirit is a man without life, love or real intelligence; without wisdom, discernment or awareness; without joy, a smile or harmony; without feeling sensitivity or friendship; without respect for life, nature or creation. Life without spirit is a life of struggle and strife in the wrong direction, filled with tension. It drains the vital living force within him and casts him onto a dark shore of loneliness. It is despair and desolation.

People without spirit are never, ever in the present. And when they are never, ever in the present, the situation will be like a puppy dog, very hungry with a bone, in a pen of hungry, wild, mentally disturbed vicious cats, who have a great hatred for dogs. Many people insist on being that little puppy dog. They go through life with suffering. To the end, they are the hard core, materialistic, greedy victims of their own whims and desires which come from the darkness and take them to that darkness.

A life of spirit is like a thousand shining suns and the smiles of heaven that reflect their magical light on the faces of a thousand white lilies, swaying on dancing, sparkling waves, with gentleness and joy, on the face of a blue lake reclining in the lap of a majestic mountain.

Life is the opportunity of all opportunities. Opportunity never waits and gives no second chances, ever. Opportunity is precious and time is a sword. If a person doesn't seize the opportunity, the time will seize him like a sharp sword and will trim his fingers, toes, arms, nose and so on. He will be running like a chicken without wings with a red hot fox running after it.

If he doesn't wake up to the real reality, he will suffer to the end of life in the phony reality of his whims, desires, ego and corroded intelligence which gets him nowhere except misery. He will be tossed relentlessly in life, just like a ship lost in a sea of terror stricken storm, forever.

Life with spirit is a life of joy, intelligence, discovery, harmony, nobility and the pathway to heaven. Not the heaven in heaven, but the heaven on earth. The intelligence is the gateway to it. There is no heaven in heaven without the heaven on earth. Heaven attracts heaven. If someone doesn't have a taste of heaven, he will never know what heaven is. As for materialistic people, how could they know of heaven when they haven't known the real taste but only the taste of fogginess, fake reality and the taste of plastic card junk.

Dry bread for a hungry man tastes like chicken without chemicals and hormones. You could obtain a chicken without chemicals and hormones from Puerto Rico or Mexico.

When the spirit is gone, the spiritless people will be gone. What is left is the form and that is a human being without essence, without awareness, without love, feeling or gentleness. He who is without the spirit is harsh, crude, rude and has no manners, conduct or good behavior. Life is meaningless, dim, gloomy, zestless. The man of this form doesn't know who he is or what is he doing. He has no heart. His mind is like a computer and he becomes a machine. He works like a machine in a heedless existence without balance.

When the spirit is gone, you are gone. So get a video and watch "Gone With the Wind," drink hot milk and make your heart warm. If you don't pass in this life, wait for the next and you will be in second grade.

When spirit is gone, the form people become deformed in their intelligence, but they don't think they are. They think they are "here," but the "here" they think of is empty, shallow, meaningless, tiring, monotonous, futile, and bogus.

The Treasure of the Spirit

The other "hereafter," the one they don't know, is real, beautiful, gentle, soft and filled with joy and love. The real "here" is the cream, the essence, the force, the strength, the sustaining, magnetic power of existence. It is the stream line that is centered on its stream.

It is the unification of mind, heart and being with the spirit. It is joy, love and peace. It is contentment, *Radha*. It is the connection to *Al Malakut,* the hidden world inside the apparent world. The hidden world is like the spirit and the apparent world is like the form. The inner world is the real and the outer world is the shadow. It is the inner world or the hidden that has the inner power that gives strength to the outer world and feeds it with the power of *Al Kayyum,* the sustaining force.

The inner power of the inner world, when it reveals itself to the one who seeks it, has a dazzling impact. It brings a powerful change to the mind, the emotion, the body and the psyche. It is like discovering a huge treasure of precious stones. It uncovers for you the hidden and unknown reality that is in truth, like nothing on earth. When you are in the reality of form, and that is the apparent world, you cannot compare it to the hidden reality.

It is like gathering all the love that exists in the world and putting it together. That love will be like a flame of fire. Nothing in it exists that is negative or jealous, suspicious or confused with anxiety. It is a complete purity and freedom, unknown on the level of a human being, but it could be known when a human being attains purity. It is possible to have glimpses of this world of magic and wonder, the world of *Al Malakut,* with certain preparation and training.

When the spirit is alive in a human being, the body or the form becomes alive with life, vivid with beauty, attractive with poise. The spirit will radiate beauty on the face and the eyes will become dark and deep like a well. It will give peace.

A human with spirit becomes balanced and his body will absorb magnetic, cosmic energy that is positive, energizing, and invigorating to all the faculties within. Its connection to the harmonious universal power will bring harmony, contentment and pleasure beyond pleasure. Most of all, he will become friends with the time and the time will become his friend. The Arabic word for friend is *sadiik.* The meaning of *sadiik* is truth and truth is one of the names of God. The time and God will be on his side. This human being will feel all the moments. Any moment in his life will then fulfill his aspirations and produce a rejoiced state.

He will be an aspiring and fulfilled human being with the truth in his heart. He will be honorable and dignified. The spirit will be his usher to the straight path, in Arabic, *Al Surat-al Mustaqueem.*

Nobility Leads to Spirit

A human without spirit is without dignity. And a human without dignity is a human without humanity. To be noble, he will be close to heaven and God loves nobility with humility. What God hates most is arrogance and lack of generosity.

The only way for humanity to thrive is with nobility. The angels of heaven will bow to a noble human and offer their services and invisibly the noble human will be elevated to higher levels. The spirit is his creative force.

A human being can impose his will on life and get the most out of life if his thoughts are directed in a positive way. Life will welcome and honor and serve him when he faces life from the fountain of spirit within. To find the fountain of spirit, he has to be a noble man with noble character. Anything short of that will keep him on the dark side of a broken reality and a confused humanity, even though this confused humanity thinks that it is fine and dandy and having a great time, thanks to the spirit that comes in bottles. May God increase the wealth of the man who puts the spirit in the bottles. Then he will put more spirit in more bottles, drink more and have more spirit.

Fish Ethic and Dry Land

The situation of this humanity is exactly like a fish who can't comprehend that there is dry land next to the water. The fish thinks that there is no such thing as dry land because he says, "I looked all over for it and I could not find it. I went down to the bottom of the sea and I dug with my tail and nose and I could not find dry land. I went all the way upstairs to the roof of the sea and I jumped above the roof and I fell down on my tummy and I got slapped. My tummy ached and I still could not find dry land. I went far and near and near and far. I could not find dry land. I asked everyone about the dry land and everyone said, "You must have had bad dreams because you are talking about something unknown, unheard of. There is no dry land and all that is there is water and the water is wet. If the water is dry, then it can't be wet. So forget about dry land. Wash your mouth with wet water, eat seaweed and wet it with wet water, that is, if you like your seaweed dinner to be wet."

But that fish had another question. He asked his mother why he had to live all of his life being wet and not dry. His mother said to him, "Why don't you go play marbles and forget about wet and dry. If Neptune hears that, he will think that you are meddling in dry magic. That is a heresy, punishable by dehydration."

This is called fish logic. Some people have similar logic when it comes to spirit. Their knowledge of spirit is not much different from the knowledge of the fish concerning the dry land or the wetness of his body and why he cannot be dry.

The Spirit as a Genie in the Bottle

A human without a spirit will depend and rely completely on all his passions, senses, emotions and expectations and the dream of his nights and the pleasure and joy of the moment and on what comes out of the bottle. What comes out of the bottle is called spirit and usually that spirit comes out at night.

The people sit around it with happy glasses. They venerate, honor and worship that spirit. Even when just looking at the bottle before the spirit bounces out, they set the stage for entertainment and contentment. In their psyche and disposition they become connected to the greatest and finest and the best pleasure given in a momentous moment, in the tide of time, in the holiest communion with the spirit that pours out or bounces out or jumps out. All the pouring, bouncing and jumping pours, bounces, and jumps in their brains. Their nervous system involuntarily starts to express the essence of the spirit when it bounces, pours, and jumps from the bottle. They become connected to the bouncing and the jumping, pouring their senses to wherever the slope of the decline takes them. Sometimes the slope ends in a gutter.

There is another kind of spirit that comes out of bottles that is completely different from the spirit just talked about. That other kind is called the spirit of the bad or, in Arabic, *efreet*. The meaning of *efreet* is genie. Also from Arabic, you could say jinn-y. Jinn-y and genie are the same.

This *efreet* wasn't following the order of King Solomon. He was the biggest, disobedient genie. And King Solomon became angry at him. He changed him to smoke and squeezed him into a bottle and sealed the bottle with the seal of King Solomon (peace be upon him). Then, King Solomon threw him in the sea, a punishment for his disobedience. This genie used to drink a lot of liquor. Solomon told him not to do it, saying, "People who drink liquor cause their brains to become smoky, foggy and polluted. They become dilapidated creatures."

So the people today should consider themselves lucky that King Solomon is not around, as there would be the greatest and biggest museum on earth that would be filled with bottles filled up with the smoke of dilapidated people.

The Wisdom of King Solomon

God gave King David wisdom. But to King Solomon, God gave wisdom with right understanding. That was very special to Solomon. King Solomon used to command all the elements of nature, the animals, the birds, the people and the jinn. He was the greatest man in the history of humanity who was given wisdom with understanding.

When King Solomon was ten years old, he was with his father, King David. Two men came to King David. One of them complained that the other man's sheep came in the night to his vineyard of grapes and ate the grapes and the vines and left nothing. He wanted the King to act on this matter. So the King's judgement was that the man with the sheep should give the sheep to the man who lost his garden.

Solomon said, "Father, I have another way concerning this matter."

And David said, "Okay, Solomon, let us hear what you have to say."

Solomon said, "The man with the sheep should give the sheep to the man who lost his grapes and vines. And the man with the sheep should take the land and grow vines and grapes on it. When they mature and give fruit, he will give the garden to its owner and then he will get his sheep back."

King David was extremely pleased with the decision of Solomon. So King David gave the title of "Wise" to Solomon and through time, Solomon has been called "Solomon the Wise," in Arabic, *Suliman Al Hakeem*.

The Junk Yard of Humanity

People without spirit will lose the knowledge of themselves. They will be incomplete and victims to their confusion. The ego will control them and the negative self will indulge in whims and desires that have no end. Dignity, honor and nobility lose ground and people become in a state of haze and daze like sleep walkers, unaware of life and reality. They exist on the outer periphery in a constant state of struggle and strife.

They become weak human beings in advanced materialistic societies that boast of great achievements in progress and civilization. They start training children to fit into the materialistic, technical, scientific systems in nursery schools. At the end of life, when they should be in the final abode of maturity, refinement, wisdom and accomplishment, they will be landing in nursing homes. This is because they put all of what they had – mentally, psychically and physically – into this technical, materialistic civilization to develop a higher and higher prosperity and prospect. They are like broken machines void of spirit, human machines that are broken and cannot be repaired. It's too late, because their abusiveness has passed the limit. A human junk yard is the dream of a materialistic, technical civilization and the spirit does not take part in it.

In a consumer society, everything will be consumed whether it is matter or a human being. It is a sorrowful ending and a disaster awaits on the corner of every block. A fine dress will end up being a rug. A fine human being will end up being a sad story to tell about the rag tag, dead, materialistic life.

When a man becomes without spirit, he will turn into an animal – heedless, without appreciation or respect for himself or for others. This great materialistic civilization will end up destroying itself by itself because when man does not use the most beautiful treasure in the universe, his intelligence, properly, the existence and the nature will destroy him. Grass will crack the cement and sprout high toward heaven to honor God and the purity of heaven.

The Meaning of "Consume"

Consumer and consume – both words carry with them a bad omen and the means of destruction and ruin, even though people rejoice in the midst of this consuming and consumption. Actually, they are destroying anything of value within them. But they bolster their weakness and shortcomings by their apparel and what they wear and how big a wardrobe they have. The bigger the wardrobe they have, the more confusion they are in. They have to clean, take care of and store and move things around in their closet and wardrobe and cabinets and drawers. Every little corner in the house is stuffed with limitless shoes and slippers. Their time has been wasted in the service of all the useless things that are hanging all over. They consume their time and also themselves.

The Webster Collegiate Thesaurus defines the word consume as "to bring to an end by, or, as if by, the action of destroying force." The example given is "The village was consumed by fire." Also, it means devour, eat up, exhaust, use up, destroy, raze, ruin, wreck, annihilate, extinguish, crush and suppress. The above words all relate and belong to consume and consumer. What these words mean is abhorrent horror. They are the final abode of consumer society.

What is really bewildering is how people are excited and overwhelmingly happy in the department stores, like a sparrow enjoying a gentle rain shower when the sun is shining at the same time. He tweets and sings on the branch of a tree. Another sparrow in a tree house that is very cozy shouts to his friend, "Sparrow Subaru, do you want an umbrella or a raincoat?"

And he says, "No thank you, Sparrow J. Crow, I don't need an umbrella or a raincoat. I am not a human being. I like my feathers to be fluffy in the air, the sun and the rain. I would be very stifled to put a coat on. These human beings, if they had feathers, would not wear a coat either."

People spend hour after hour, day after day, year after year, to no end, in offices, shoveling and shuffling paper after paper. This goes on and on forever. These papers, at the most, deal with dead content and matter that causes the essence in a human being to be dehydrated. Those human beings try to gain back their essence by eating and drinking. They are in a state of negative anxiety and their minds have been twisted from confusion just like a tornado hitting a shanty village. The nervousness and tension does not let them be calm and see things as they are. They resort to eating and drinking the worst food and drink, eating and drinking without distinction. Because when they are confused, the negative self thrives, rejoices and becomes extremely happy. The ego becomes in command and any sensibility or reasoning is blown away with the tornado. They eat and drink anything they can get their hands on. The supermarket is the heaven and paradise for the negative self, the ego, the desires and the whims. When people are in that state and are in the supermarket, they look like the underworld of creatures from the Planet of the Apes. To bolster their twisted mentality, when at the cashier's stand, there are magazines and publication headlines that the devil would be horrified to glimpse. One of the magazines has a picture of a two headed baby with a caption that reads, *"Eleven year old girl gives birth to alien."* This shows what kind of a state the publisher, the editor, the story writer and the people who read this material are in. And on and on it goes.

Trash Thought in a Trash Bag

It is the degenerate mentality of human beings who forget that they are human beings and that they are created for a better purpose in life and not to waste their time in nonsensical, meaningless and stupid pursuits. Thoughts that are equal to trash make their thinker a bag of trash. The trash thoughts in the bag never know what are clean and beautiful thoughts. It is only a derangement in the mind that leads a human being to be twisted in his thought and to lose connection with his essence and reality.

A thought could be dark and project a dark reality of ignorance and confusion, while a bright beautiful thought projects bright, light reality with delight and harmony. The hidden secret behind these two states is the presence or absence of spirit. If the spirit is there, you are in the light, bright reality. If the spirit is not there, you are in the dark and miserable reality. So hold on to the spirit. Seek the spirit and your life will be like a bright star. A peace of the paradise of heaven will come down to you, to surround you and to be your environment. The spirit gives you what no man without spirit would think or dream of.

Have no spirit and your life will be like a dog. You will sweat and toil to no end. You will suffer through the life even if you drink all the liquor in the world, all the wine, all the beer, all the cocaine, all the soft drinks, all the cake, all the chocolate and all the junk food. None of these will help you or show you happiness and contentment.

When you drink, you imagine that you are content and happy. That is only an illusion which destroys the beautiful faculties within you as a human being. Don't cheat and fool yourself or make believe. When you do the wrong things, you amount to nothing more than an animal, without honor, without dignity, without imagination and without love. You will arrive at your grave sweating and toiling and that is the end of it. So if you never came to this world and you did not exist, it would be better than to exist without knowing who you are, without knowing how to live in peace and how to enjoy all the beautiful days that make the life beautiful and filled with the eternal light.

The Wrong Civilization

It seems the more people advance in a wrong civilization, the more confusion takes place. It is like a huge octopus getting hold of the essence of a human being and destroying him. In a wrong civilization, plastic, chemical and junk food becomes the delight and the joy of the day and the night. The more people eat this kind of food, the more they poison themselves. Liquor and drugs offer nothing for them except to be drugged in a destructive way. Then you have a drugged society with destroyed brains and people going around without knowing what is going on.

What is a wrong civilization? A wrong civilization is a civilization that has no consciousness, is based on the ego and intellectual hypothesis, and has no discernment or awareness. Monopoly, greed, and competition are looked up to as holy covenants. A wrong civilization is wrong when it is divested of spirit. It is not real. It is phony — gratification of the senses is the ultimate.

The department stores are the mecca where people go to pay homage to one more shirt or a plastic duck. I assure you, even if those people wear golden clothes, it will do them no good because when the spirit is dead, the person is dead.

Someone said in the Middle East, *"If you have no spirit, you will taste bitter even if you smear your body with honey."*

When the spirit is dead, you are a form that is lost wherever you are or wherever you go. You have no connection to the source of life or to the reality. You are isolated from the essence within you and outside of you. The brainless material imposes its will upon you. What an amazing, bewildering and baffling situation this is. Material which has no brain controls a man that has a brain, and that is a man with intelligence, reasoning, senses, and imagination — a man who thinks, talks and converses. A man with all of these faculties goes down the drain and becomes deranged when the material controls him. A man who is born free becomes enslaved to material that doesn't know what is going on.

The only reason that man loses all the great and marvelous faculties and goes to the lowest of the low is that he disassociates himself from the grandest thing in existence, his spirit. When the spirit is gone, a man is lost like a lost little kitten on a rainy, stormy night in an area that is infested with dogs, coyotes, wolves and a lunatic Godzilla.

What the Junk Says to Man

So let all those spiritless people buy more and more useless junk. It will not be too long before they will be junk sitting amidst the junk they acquired. They will become worried to think of moving away from it because junk and material are their masters. The junk and material don't know, and will never know, that they are the masters and that man is the slave because junk and material have no say in the matter. The mastery is imposed on them by the man when the man has no spirit. When the man has no spirit, he will be a complete moron and the stupidest creature that ever walked the face of the earth since the Stone Age and up to the fringes of the Space Age.

A man who is obsessed by junk and material will become junk. When he is sitting among his junk, if he moves away, he will hear a voice in his head, projected from the junk, shouting and reprimanding him in a loud voice, *"Where are you going, stupid?! Sit Down. Who is going to watch us? You are junk and your place is with junk and as long as you have no spirit, you are not worth a penny."* And a fear will take over the man. He will tremble and worry about the junk, especially when the junk speaks the truth.

Junk goes to junk and spirit goes to spirit. In the spirit, there is life. When the life has spirit, the life has love. When the life has love, heaven smiles at you. The spirit rejoices with the sunset and the perfumed roses, and life fulfills its destiny every moment of the day or night.

With the spirit, you are in harmony with existence. You are in unity with the beautiful reality and the sun fills your heart with joy and light. The moon fills your imagination with dreams that are carried on the wings of the spirit of heaven. You and the heaven are connected with the bond of *sala*. *Sala*, in Arabic, means relationship of enticing leisure and nobility.

Materialistic people adamantly refuse to use their brains in a positive way. God gives you a brain and with it you could transform your existence to a higher existence. But when you choose the material and discard the spirit, you become weak, sick, confused, tense and nervous. You find contentment and joy in liquor, drugs, smoke and junk food. Your face becomes gloomy, never knowing the joy of a smile. Your eyes have a plastic look, your being, a withered countenance, and negative energy radiates from your face.

When everyone in the society has the same symptoms, then the damnation and the curse of God becomes lawful to destroy the people who have no regard for all the fabulous things that are given freely to them. The air, the light, the sun, the elements, the plants, the animals — all are offered on a golden platter to man, but man turns around and throws all these things in the gutter. And his turn will come to be thrown in the gutter.

When the Spirit is Chewed

In a consumer society, spirit is chewed in factories, offices, department stores, shops, night clubs and topless bars, where people lose the tops of their heads and their brains become topless. They are polluted with smoke, smog and hazy, dazy thoughts that make them anxious and confused. Just as a man chews tobacco and spits it out, the same thing happens in a consumer society. They chew their spirit and spit it out.

Be a seeker of your intelligence and not your intellect. Be a worshipper of your intelligence and not your emotion. Be a slave to your intelligence and not to your sensuality and heaven will tell the inner cosmic reality, the hidden, marvelous beauty of existence and nature, *Al Jamal,* to be a friend to you. This produces a reality of true reality, a reality of magic, marvel and wonder, a reality of life and love in natural unity and harmony.

In the true reality, there is nothing but pleasure, refinement, and contentment and there is never room in it for a speck of anything unpleasant. You are on the top of this world that you are in. You are inside the hidden world of the reality that is completely unknown to the people who are drifters and wanderers with no focus or keen perception of anything. They only worry about the past and what is going to happen in the future. Between the future and the past, they are lost in a maze that has no present. The past is already lost and the future is not here and the present has no present. This is the lost link between the beginning and the end. And there is no connection to the time whether past, future or now. A person in that state truly does not exist. He does not know the meaning of life and he does not know the meaning of a human being or what is a human being.

Is man a machine, a tool, an object, or an animal without a brain? That is what man is when he is divested of spirit, when he is without will, discipline and determination and follows his ego's wish like wood drifting on a wave. The ego's wishes will take him from darkness to darkness – the whims are fatal blows to the spirit.

Soul and Reward

The Koran said, *"Each soul is rewarded according to its deeds."*

Perfection is an ultimate purpose by itself and whatever you see in this world comes from perfection. Man can be part of that perfection if he goes first to the depth within himself, to his consciousness, imagination, being, heart, spirit and soul. When he goes to that depth, powerful tools like perception, understanding, awareness, discernment, and pure intelligence, which is the bridge or the connection to the outer realm and the path, pours the light of heaven into his heart and his eyes.

The ultimate purpose and goal of man is evolution and perfection. When he achieves that, he will be a true *khalifa*, or representative of God on earth. When man becomes complete or perfect, he is in a wakeful state. The nature of the wakeful state is a binding, natural relationship between man, existence, the universe and God. A beautiful relationship based on the unwritten covenant between man and God.

The spirit has a powerful magnetic attraction known in Arabic as *Al Jathb*. That power only operates in the realm of spirit. Spirit attracts spirit. That attraction is beyond intellect, emotion, sensuality and the physical. It operates in the highly developed reality and truth of the spirit. The spirit is what makes life beautiful. Without the spirit, you have a life, but it has no happiness.

80CB

You Reap Poison
If You Sow It

God created man that he might worship. The Arabic word for worship is *abadah*. The *abadah* has no limit. It is like the number "one," where all the numbers come from and it has no end. *Abadah* is the same. The beginning of it starts on earth and is the love that radiates peace. The other side of it is in Heaven and is the multiplication of the love on earth.

The true worship is love. Until people understand this simple matter, their worship will be filled with fear, reservation and apprehension and they will be in the darkness of the heart, mind and spirit. In that darkness, they carry a lighted matchstick to see their way in the darkness, unaware of *Al Noor*, the light of Heaven that fills the universe.

The matchlight actually, is material and technology, created with the little flickering brains of the materialistic people, which make them so proud of their accomplishments. But their accomplishments have no worth or value because they come from dead spirit which kills them in the end. A mouse who eats poison will die. And you reap what you sow.

෨෬

If people know the tranquility, the contentment, and the depth of love which fill all the space and come from the spirit, they will leave all the nonsensical things and be in love with the spirit.

Man and Spirit

In man there is a spirit that comes from pure source. But when the mind is not balanced, the material and the mind pushes the spirit away and opens the way to anxiety, confusion, greed, conflict, and strife. The limited intellect, when the spirit is not part of it, will not be able to see what is missing in life.

Men drive on wheels. The more they drive, the farther away they get from the spirit. The farther they get from well-being, the more their faces assume the look of a bat in the dark! But the bat has more peace in his heart than the man who has lost his spirit. And the farther away from the spirit, the smaller the mind will be and the greater the pride.

Confusion and stupidity are the result of lost spirit and a nervous life becomes set around the man. He becomes a machine. When he is in the laundry, he is a machine with machines! There is no difference from machine to machine. His value becomes the value of a machine. His voice becomes a mechanical voice because love has died in his heart. He becomes emotionally confused. He becomes half alive and half dead. The living part of him becomes mentally, psychically, emotionally and physically stiff and sick. This is the lowest of the low among human beings who are absolutely incapable of knowing who they are.

It all depends on the individual and what he makes of his life. Either he can make it as good as heaven or as bad as hell. It all depends on the thought, the intention, the desire, the will, the discipline, a refined disposition, and an intense high purpose in life, to volunteer the life to good deeds, to make the life part of a whole. Go through life seeking the higher, the better, the real, the beautiful, and the meaningful life, when life and truth accept each other. Truth becomes life and life becomes truth. And heaven and earth bind and hold each other in a unity which can only be known to the life that is submerged in the true reality. Truth becomes the face of manifested existence.

When selfishness and greed become part of creativity, creativity becomes a form without spirit. Spiritless creativity leads to the damnation of man and man becomes a creature that looks like a human being, but is without the essence of a human being. He is more like a fish, unwanted by the sea and discarded by the sea onto the shore of loneliness, the shore of darkness, even if the sun is as bright as all the light of heaven. The fish is on land with artificial breathing and artificial legs.

And a cat smells the fish and loves the smell of the fish, because the smell of the fish gives the cat a great appetite. And the cat is dying to eat a fish. The cat is thinking and getting nervous and tense over whether to eat the fish starting with the tail or the head. But the interest of the cat is in the flesh. The cat actually represents the negative self and the negative self wants to eat the man alive. It is prime time for the cat to eat the fish. And any time is prime time for gluttony.

When the senses are in command, they will dwarf the spirit and push it away as if it never existed. When the man is in a heedless, forgetful state and unaware of the beautiful reality, then regardless of how much he achieves in the development of material and progress, he lives only in the outer dark slum fringes of a make believe reality. That reality is the result of abusing the great faculties within him like the mind, the intelligence, the senses, the emotions, the body, the feeling, the imagination, the creativity, the innovation, the determination, the discipline, and the will.

These are all powerful tools to develop and bring the spirit to the realm of life, love and transcendence and to higher spheres of discovery, contentment and peace. If these tools are used improperly, instead of getting the spirit, the man will be like the fish out of water and the cat will chase him forever. Even if the cat does not catch him, anxiety, problems and tension will dehydrate his brain and his body will be shrivelled like a dead battery without juice. He will be fit only for a museum of antiquity, to stand next to a mummy from a Mexican pyramid which is in an extremely bad state of wrapping.

Ignorance of the self marks the borderline between heaven and hell. If you know the self or part of the self or are relatively acquainted with the self, you are in heaven while you are on earth. If you don't know the self, you are in hell while you are on earth.

It is all in the thought. When the thought is instigated by the negative thought with the blessing of the negative self, the negative self creates a picture of delight for all the things that will lead you to misery and strife. Not for a moment will it let you think you are anywhere but in the right place and that you are doing fine, even though you are in the lowest of low places.

Today is the most important day of your life. If the thought in your head is positive and connected to the spirit within you, you become connected to the day that is in your hand, not the day of yesterday or the day of tomorrow. The day that is in your hand becomes vibrant, still, settled and also innovative and creative, rich with the essence of creation, and the abundant living force and energy. This day is a day that comes to you from heaven. It has the leisure of heaven and the joy of paradise. So respect this day and give it its due appreciation, honor and value. Your face will be a mirror to reflect the beauty, charm and magic of the creation when your heart, your mind, your love, and your existence are in unity with the essence of heaven and earth. This day holds the secret of beautiful knowledge, the inner knowledge of the self, a knowledge that has never existed in a book which has been written by man when man does not know who he is. Inner knowledge or self knowledge is a direct experience with reality and the cosmos.

If you use your intelligence properly, without building your reality around the senses as if they are the sole purpose in your life, then the real truth becomes apparent to you. Life becomes charming and tranquil and unity with the creation becomes possible when you go to the hidden light that is imbedded in the time and in the inner intelligence of the heart.

ॐ

Beautiful thoughts originate in heaven and the person who has them is beautiful. Ugly thoughts originate in a deep, dark abyss, never knowing light or air and the person who has them is ugly and repulsive.

Holy Rabbit and Civilization

The greatest feat of the materialistic age is to keep the feet on the accelerator and the brake and away from dirt. This has resulted in weak ankles, loose calves, flabby thighs, shaky buttocks, overwhelming fat in general, big bellies in particular, and tension in the nervous system. The nervous system can not handle the constant impact of the speed and highways. The face assumes a confused, tense look and the smile dies away, so that even Charlie Chaplin will not be able to restore it.

The imagination of these people is like a cat's imagination. And the imagination of cats is all about mice. But they are not supposed to eat mice, because they are people. So they settle for hot dogs. The big billboard says, "World's biggest hot dog, made of selected ingredients to enhance the bud of your taste and your health. Eat it and it will put a broad smile on your face. It will restore your nervous system with a new kick and it will put pink color on your cheeks. Your cheeks will look like two rosebuds that are coming into bloom and life."

The pink color will make you look healthy, even though your lungs are black like the tar of the highway when it is hot. They pour it to make more highways which your car runs on while you are not running. Your legs become weak like dwindling spaghetti, because they are not engaging in action as God intended them to do. That is the reason why they become weak like spaghetti. So you have to be very, very protective of them. And never, never, ever have a nap in a park when you get dizzy from breathing the smog. This is truly a most serious warning involving a most serious matter in your life that could cripple you forever, and never, never, ever would you be able to drive or walk again.

The Spirit in the Rabbit

Now, I will tell you the nature of that serious warning. It is about a hippie who spent many years searching for the truth in India. He found it in a statue of a little rabbit by the name of God Rabbit Raton Koo KahKooKoo, who is supposed to be one of the ancient gods of lust and quick desires, of gluttony and hedonistic practices including the chocolate bar and apple pie. And spaghetti is a must.

So this hippie came back with a long list of reforms and long hair that is not supposed to be washed, to keep up with the trend and the mode of the new age and also to keep a manly, natural look and to keep his fingernails long so the dirt under them will look black to give them a raggedy-taggedy and original look. And this is to bolster the image of spiritual evolution and to be in opposition to the red, gold, pink, and green fingernail polish and the other shades of fingernail polish and never to visit beauty salons because it will weaken the spirit and will detract from the veneration, adoration, devotion and ritual of burning tons of incense until you become insane and smoking tons of hash until you become numb in your brain, tongue, heart, liver, kidney and extremities. All this was for the little rabbit God Rabbit Raton Koo KahKooKoo.

Our hippie, who came back from India with a rabbit in his bag for a god, came back with a new name that gave him aloofness, high stature, airiness and commendable dignity that would give him the upper hand in implementing a new way to spirit in this viciously spiritless and corrupt system of material that changes people from beautiful human beings into being like a lunatic duck that swims in the sand because of water phobia.

Spirit or Devil in the Eyes

No one looks anyone in the eyes, because their spirit is dead. Instead of seeing the spirit in the eyes, they see the devil in the eyes. That is what frightens them. Even though they can't look at the devil in their eyes, they deal with each other as a devil. In a society of devils, drugs, liquor and addiction are the controlling tools of the devil. More and more, society is creating new laws to combat the activities of the devil and more and more people find new loopholes to break the laws.

New laws are not the answer. The answer is to kill the devil within and to crown the spirit as king, with all the royal regalia. A king who is a man with spirit will bring heaven to earth. God said in the Koran, *"Man's dealing with man may be a source of bliss and joy."* This saying could come true in societies of tension and anxiety in the western world that are unjustly labeled civilization.

Materialistic man thinks he is very advanced in culture and civilization. He drives a car on tar while his forefathers used to walk on dirt. They did not know the word "psychologist." The doctor was not a common thing, nature was their doctor. They were happy and content. They never, ever worried about finding change in dimes and nickels for the dumbest and most stupid creation of the so-called civilized man, the parking meter.

One civilized man put a quarter in the meter and went to buy a baseball hat. When he came back he saw Mr. Metermaid about to write a ticket. The man said, "Well, I just put a quarter in the meter, you know and I just came back to put in another."

But Mr. Metermaid said, "Oh, it is too late! You broke the law and it is too late. And all of us have to be diligent in being careful not to break the law."

So the hippie with the rabbit for a god in his bag chose the name Guru Penjali Paharaji Pahdari Bahrori, Guard and

Keeper of the Temple of God Rabbit Raton Koo KahKooKoo and Keeper of the most Secret of Secrets, of the greatest phenomenal secret that ever came out of India and landed on the shores of this spiritually barren land. This consciously burned out terrain has nothing to do with, nor knows anything about the spirit. But maybe the spirit has to do with Robin Hood and stealing the golden plate of the Sheriff of Nottingham and selling it to the moneylender. And with the money he gets, he showers a poor bride and groom with the coins, instead of rice.

Coyote, Indians and Cowboys

This land is deprived of the spirit, so permanently burned out from the spirit, it is like the Sahara Desert which has never seen one single drop of water in a thousand years. That takes it all the way back to the red Indians, who taught some spiritually deprived cowboys how to smoke, chew and eat tobacco. They taught cowboys how to mix peyote with buffalo hamburger and to eat it, to soothe the kidneys and to be serene and to conduct serene deals with the Indians, like giving the Indians guns and getting whatever they wanted from them.

When the cowboys used peyote, they started hallucinating. They saw a coyote standing on his legs, shouting and saying to them, "You are all sinners for drinking whiskey and fighting with each other like lunatics. The wolves behave better than you. They have better manners than you. They sit in a counsel and discuss their affairs. They kiss each other on the cheeks. Then they have dinner in a most gentle, civilized way that would seem a model for you to learn from and to study the democracy of the wolves.

"If you don't get rid of your sins, you will be a nonsense scrabble. You will be put in hell fire. And the only way out of it is to stop drinking whiskey and to start drinking coyote milk! And then howl like a coyote!"

Then all the cowboys started howling like coyotes. They said to the coyote, "You are our God. We believe in you and no other god comes anywhere near you, even if they come from India as a rabbit god. But tell us a wise word from your wisdom. Which supermarket carries coyote milk? And what is your advice for nonfat milk or fat milk?"

Coyote said, "It is not in a supermarket! A supermarket product is all poison and all the people who eat the product will be filled with poison. They will be sick and permanent diseases will be with them. It is a slow suicide. Those people will feel miserable, unhappy, sad and filled with fear — all of that because some men are greedy and selfish. They use chemicals in apples to make them bigger to make more money. Then they kill the people with the apples."

Jesus said, "Do unto others as you would have them do unto you."

Then the coyote said to get coyote milk from the teepee of Chiquita Rosa Maria, near the cave of the Holy White Eagle.

Penjali and the Secret of Pleasure

Hippie Guru Penjali is the short name he uses to make it easy for conversation, because he found that when he told them all the name, they would spend two hours figuring it out, instead of doing the headstand, which he brought with him from India, the greatest secret of them all, the holy of holies, the liberating secret of liberation, the hidden power that will bring leisure and pleasure, the secret that will bring not only the knowledge of the self and the knowledge of God, but also the knowledge of reincarnation, and the knowledge of who is who, and the knowledge of where was it, and the knowledge of was it or wasn't it, and the knowledge of cookware, and whether tandoori oven bread tastes better than electric oven bread, and which of those breads brings the third eye to a better focus.

So, you not only have the secret of all this knowledge, but also you will discover the secret of how to maintain a high, holy look. Wherever you turn, you will look holy, as if in a lofty place of spirit that you never, never come down from. And when you are in the never-never-ever-come-down-from-it state, then you could eat all and everything, be it Coca Cola, whiskey, Dr. Pepper, RC Cola, tequila, beer, Jolt with double the sugar and double the jolt, coffee, milkshakes, chocolate (either Swiss or English), Chinese cookies, pizza, stuffed pig, big and curled pork rind, sugar and gelatin candies and whatever your whims, heart, and desires are asking of your negative self. Your ego will say "Oh boy, I love it all, give me more, even cocaine, heroin, hash and marijuana."

The Secret of the Rabbit

Now I am going to tell you the secret (and you could tell it to anyone you wish) in very plain language. And those with intelligence will know it very quickly. Those without intelligence will never know it, even if they record it on tape as a song and play it day and night to themselves.

People are either born intelligent or born stupid — there is no power on earth that could change this. Some adjustments could be made with stupid people, but nothing can be done with their essence, because stupid people have no essence. Some conduct, behavioral conditions and habits could be taught and they will respond to it. But these are mechanical changes that will not affect them deep within. The center of emotion could be activated and used to induce practices to bring about change. But the power of real love cannot be affected, because that is the missing focus of those people.

Now I will explain the secret of the rabbit, His Holiness, the Archduke of Wisdom and the Sea of Knowledge, the Mountain of Words of Pearls and the River of Information, His Excellency, Rabbit God Raton Koo KahKooKoo, who is a real god who lived in India five thousand years ago and who is still alive and manifests himself in person to the one who has faith and belief in him. This is how you do it to have Rabbit God Raton Koo KahKooKoo come to you in person:

Wake up at three o'clock in the morning. Take an ice cold bath by filling half the tub with ice and the other half with water. Lay in it or in between it without hesitation. With courage and magnanimity, shout in a loud voice, Koo Ka Koo Koo Koo Koo. Kick and hit the ice with your hands and say, "Oh ice, be hot and warm on me."

According to a story in the Koran, when people wanted to burn Prophet Abraham, they put him in the fire. But God said to the fire, "Oh fire, be cold and peaceful."

The second thing to do, after your bout with the ice, is to do the hula dance in your underwear. The third thing to do is to wear a fluffy robe and a turban that is ten times bigger than your head. Wear two earrings, each one weighing a ton and a ring on your nose that overwhelms your lips. When you talk, the ring will be between the lips and will produce a whistling sound that has a passionate and telepathic effect on the spirit.

To Rabbit God Raton Koo KahKooKoo, light many candles and a lot, a lot of incense. Put Christmas lights around his temple and in front of his statue a lot of carrots and cucumbers with strawberries for dessert. Wear bells around your waist, around your neck, around your wrists and ankles and across your shoulders, just like Pancho Villa when he wore the bullets across his shoulders. But your purpose will be different than Pancho Villa's, and bells have a more charming sound than bullets.

The fourth thing to do is to lay on the ground on your tummy in front of the statue God Rabbit Raton Koo KahKooKoo. Ask for forgiveness and ask him to give you a red convertible Cadillac with a kitchenette on one side, a music deck and a little oven in which to bake hot pie on the other. Then you will have fresh, hot pie and a little refrigerator for milk, to soothe the taste of the hot apple pie. And vanilla ice cream is favorable, also.

The fifth thing to do is to stand up, shake all the bells, dance, jump up and down and go into a convulsive action of hysterical movement and shout, "God Raton, come to me and give me enlightenment! Take me to heaven! I am sick and tired of this consumer society which has no purpose in life except to drink beer and watch television. They hate what they do in their work and they say there is nothing else to do."

When you finish that, the sixth thing to do is to sit cross legged and fix your eyes on the nose of the rabbit. Do that for eight hours without deviating your sight from the tip of the nose. You will find the rabbit winking his eyes, left and right and lifting his eyebrows, alternately up and down and wiggling his moustache. He will be making faces at you. If you laugh, all the action in the face of the rabbit will stop and you will lose the connection. But if you are very serious and keep straight face, then the rabbit will manifest himself and come out of the statue. He will lick you all over and you will become enlightened.

If you wish by then, you have two choices. One is to stay as you are and the other is that he will transform you into a statue of a rabbit. Then, you will become another Rabbit God Raton Koo KahKooKoo and you will never have to take ice cold baths anymore. And you will be liberated from the hustle and bustle of life. And you don't even have to hustle your nose.

The Dream of Tomato Paste

Now let us go back to the warning. As I said, it is the most important and serious warning in all your life and existence. It involves the hippie who came back from India. He had a dream while in India. He was told in the dream to carry with him a can of tomato paste and a bottle of ketchup. When he is going home, while travelling, he will come to a road side park on the highway. In the park, he will see a man sleeping, completely exhausted from breathing the smog and he'll be wearing shorts. His legs will look like dwindling spaghetti. While he is asleep, the hippie is to pour the tomato paste and the ketchup on his legs and start eating them in a hurry.

Now this is why I said the warning is important. To save your spaghetti legs, stop wearing shorts and wear long baggy pants stuffed with rubber. Stop working on a pig farm and sleep there, then you don't need to drive anymore. You will save a lot of money by not buying gas. And with that money, you could always buy a pig. Then, you could eat all day long, especially in the evening. Eat a leg of pig every day and your legs will be fat like a pig's and no more like loose spaghetti. But be careful not to become fat like a pig.

In advanced materialistic societies, some of the people glorify material and lose their glory as human beings. They become faded human beings. They become more machines than the machines they operate. They become office junkies, factory junkies, shop junkies and junkies wherever they are. They are not sound human beings. They have lost the spark of a human being which comes from the vital force of life. Then the vital force of life has lost its vitality and becomes more dead than alive. Doing all the wrong things causes them to be mechanical and not spontaneous human beings. They become dull, without charm or a smile. They have lost the connection to the natural nature in the heart of human beings. They have lost the spark of humanity which is as bright in the face as the bright sun. What is left is a withering dullness, without even a dim flicker of candlelight as a reminder.

It is possible to correct this miserable situation if a man starts doing the right things. But if a man thinks being in a bar every single night is beautiful, then anxiety and tension will be his companion and the spark of life will never come near him. When people become machines they will lose their discernment, understanding and distinction. They won't be able to distinguish between a man and a pig.

Now the warning about the man with the loose spaghetti legs is very valid here again for you. When working at the pig farm, don't get as fat as a pig! Because some people will come to the farm and buy and slaughter a pig. And if you are as fat as a pig, they will cut you and slaughter you and eat you. They can't tell the difference between you as a man or a pig, even if you scream and your voice goes to heaven. Your screaming might make them admire your scream. They will say, "What a beautiful loud squeak, which whets our appetite. A loud, squealing pig is a sign of a healthy pig!"

ಬಂ

Do one thing wrong and it will lead to another wrong and the wrong things will multiply and soon you will drown in a sea of wrong things.

Vultures of Technology

Materialistic people choke their spirit with material that they think is important to their bliss and happiness. But, their spirit becomes like a cement block reinforced with steel and the spirit becomes dead. In this case, whatever is around the spirit of the finest material, including the body, becomes trash and reflects the death of spirit. Anxiety, tension, confusion, sadness and life without happiness, wisdom or intelligence becomes their lot, even if they sit on a sofa that is made of solid gold upholstery with the finest satin or velvet. They will be no more than vultures feasting on a carcass of dead, stinking fish.

Material and technology without spirit will turn people into animals without brains. Material and technology become the curse of heedless people, when technology does not have the spirit as its base. Any development in the life of people that is void of spirit is a vain, wasteful, useless, senseless, lost reality. This development has no imagination or love and is in a state of darkness and ignorance.

When the spirit disintegrates, the ego will be its replacement. The character and ideal of the ego is selfishness, greed, jealousy, hate, suspicion, anxiety, tension, confusion, ignorance, constriction, vanity and a dark psyche. Paranoia is the cream that tops all of these delightful traits. And you could have your treat with cream or without it, if you are conscious of sugar and do not want to get fat.

There is a subtle connection between trait and treat. It is thin like a thread, but it binds them together like a Persian carpet. Whatever your trait, it will look for its kind of treat and whatever the treat, it will look for its kind of trait. If your trait is inclined toward spirit, you will look for treats to enhance the spirit, like going to a movie that inspires you to do good deeds. But if your trait is inclined toward the ego, you will go to a movie filled with violence, crime and confusion and you will be inspired toward corruption. If you have a little sense left in your head, you should go and study Confucianism to get rid of your confusion.

There is a good deal of measurement between opposites, like day and night, enlightenment and ignorance, intelligence and stupidity, dense stone and fluid water, open heartedness and closed heartedness and Confucianism and confusion. If you use your intelligence properly, you will pick up on all the opposites that lead to harmony, peace and bliss. If you are able to project just a tiny little bliss in yourself, then the bliss of heaven will rain and shower on you. It will be as if you are in a garden of perfumed roses.

When life has no spirit, it will be empty and shallow like a desert that hasn't seen rain in a thousand years. When people have no spirit and don't know how to get the spirit, they will be lost in a dark existence, even under the light of the sun. Their brains become constricted. They become weak, nervous and tense.

They become like machines working hard to fit and compliment the technology. They don't have the slightest idea of what they are doing or why.

The only thing they know they want is to be happy, content and to have a good time. They will die without knowing the real contentment, happiness or good times. They only know fake, phony, unreal happiness. They imagine that the liquor, the drugs and the processed food filled with chemicals and poison are the real causes of happiness, contentment and good times. This fabricated happiness, in truth, is a slow suicide.

But they are already dead, because when the body is filled up with poison and the mind with illusion, people cannot think straight. If they don't think straight, their thinking is vain and in vain simultaneously. Their thoughts become

41

slimy and creepy like a snail who has never seen the light of the sun and prefers to be under humid, damp dirt and breathes the dirt to get high. To the snail, where it's at is the whole world.

When people lose the connection to reality, their spirit is lost. Tension, gloom, complaints and worry become their normal state. They will sink in existence in a mile-deep, dark ditch, with no rope or ladder to get out. They have mistaken the relative for the real. An example of that is in their work in offices where they shovel paper and fill drawer after drawer and shelf after shelf and room after room with papers. They gather data and information about dumb, stupid, nonsensical things and keep an account of every little dime and nickel.

This is truly an inverted, confused case of humanity which has lost its senses and has mistaken the shoveling of papers for the highest cause in life. This is truly the lost cause of people who are ignorant of themselves. They devote their entire life to the cause of shoveling papers. Each year they have only two weeks vacation. To have two weeks vacation and to work the rest of the year is completely wrong and unjust to the self, to humanity, to consciousness, to the spirit, to the reality and to heaven and to earth. Those people accomplish nothing of value or dignity. They kill the real aspiration for the real knowledge, *ma'arifa*, which is the knowledge of the self.

The Koran said, "Man is born to learn," and that means to learn about the self. All other learning that people do in the world, studying and in colleges combined is secondary to the knowledge of the self. You could learn everything and excel in it and be the master of it and have a dozen doctorate degrees, but without the knowledge of the self, you are as ignorant as a frog who cannot comprehend the horse or the purpose of the horse or why the hoof of the horse is deadly when it steps on a frog.

In order for people without spirit to remedy the situation, they should get together in the evening, sing like frogs and drink spirit in the form of whiskey. This is an alternative and substitute which will put them to sleep, a dark state of sleep. The opposite of the dark, extremely dense state of sleep is a vibrant state of sleep actually unknown to the people, but it can be done and it has been done with the appropriate knowledge. The vibrant sleep is light, bright and in a wakeful state. It combines sleep and wakefulness at the same time. It is restful, beautiful, invigorating, inspiring and rich. It makes you creative and content.

When people who shovel papers, and you could call them "Paper Shovelers," get old, they die and leave all the paper they shoveled behind them. No one will look at these papers until the end of the world and the papers will live happily ever after. If those ignorant people who shovel papers all their lives knew better, they would jump rope, play with tame rabbits in green meadows, roll on the grass, dance and exclaim, "I love green grass!" At least they could breathe good fresh air and they would have strong bodies, be smiling and have shining eyes. And that is better than to work like a dog.

Of course, the dog never works. Especially if the work is nonsense. All the dog will do is tear the papers to protest the shoveling. That is an indication for intelligent human beings to learn from the dog. Of course, a shepherd dog works, but his work is play and sport. He is enjoying nature, the meadow, the hills, the trees, the blue sky, the sun, the breeze and the company of sheep and lambs. He runs, jumps, friskily rolls on his back and artistically and precisely, without reservation, growls and sings, thinking he is an opera singer. In a most positive way, he entertains himself and the baby lambs who frolic, jump and bounce around him in complete freedom, wondering about this creature who looks different from the sheep. And he is happy and jolly. They admire his singing, trying to imitate him with their soft, tender and gently shrieking voices.

The shepherd dog loves what he is doing, whether you call it work or play. There is no boundary or definite line between the two. The dog is present with his heart, mind, feeling, the environment, the nature and the creation, all in the moment. Because of which, any work he does, whether hard or easy, doesn't matter. All will be fine, fun, play and pleasure.

When you are in connection with anything that you do, with all your concentration, feeling and imagination, whatever you do becomes a prayer more powerful than prayer — a prayer of essence and creativity which finds its way to the positive reality. The cosmic energy will come to assist you and make what you are doing more sweet than honey and the blessing of heaven will pave your way with roses.

When work becomes beneficial to you and to other people and has essence within it to improve the situation by bringing evolution and progress, that kind of work is real work. Its blueprint is found in the spirit. Its harmony penetrates the element in the existence. It creates a communication between the work accomplished and the surroundings in a harmonious celebration that binds the perfection of what is accomplished with the nature.

As the great master Ibn 'Ata'illah said, "Work and deeds are forms that exist. Its spirit is the secret loyalty in it."

Of course, this cannot be applied to a mass consumer production that has no connection between the work and the workers. The real connection in this situation is the money and how much money the workers will be making by offering so much work. That is the cause of confusion, unhappiness and misery.

Technology without spirit obliterates intelligence and makes the brain lower than a monkey's brain. When a person's brain becomes lower than a monkey's brain, the person will look up to the monkey as a symbol between him and the missing truth. So, he sits in front of the monkey. It is no wonder to see a person, with a mentality lower than a monkey's, venerating, paying homage, respecting, praying and worshipping a monkey. The dream of a monkey is a ripe banana. The human being, who is created with the highest faculty in creation and who is created for a higher destiny, will lower himself below the monkey. May God save spiritless technology, the great heritage of humanity, until everyone is a monkey. And the monkey says, "Life is nothing but a banana. To be in a banana boat is the dream of eternity and the quest of monkey civilization."

ॐ

How To Put Spirit In Matter

When the materialistic man's mind gets veiled from the truth, he will be incapable of seeing the simple, sweet reality. His mind becomes mingled and shingled with ignorance and becomes protected from any light that might disperse the darkness in the mind of this materialistic man. He will be driving, without a real purpose, on highways to no good end. His mingled mind drives him to a dead future, even though he thinks that he is an evolved human being with a highly developed civilization which is running on wheels. He is sitting on the wheels all his life, going and coming, back and forth, until his body becomes stiff and wired. And he becomes the wired connection to his car.

Good deeds make a man perfect. If he does not do good deeds, he will be imperfect. Imperfection is the result of bad deeds that come from heedlessness and not having understanding or appreciation of any certain situation.

Perfection makes a human being perfect and beautiful. Any perfection without spirit will lead to ugliness and misery. To seek perfection in the self, in others, in life, in nature and in whatever you do, will enliven your days and make the world around you beautiful.

If a human being seeks perfection in the world of material, he will open the door to the world of spirit. But to open the world of spirit, he needs faith in himself and in his spirit. A miracle will take place from just the right thought. Mohammad said, "If you do any work, perfect it and God will love you."

When material or objects are put together, whether in art or created work, they will come to a complete balance if the material or the objects are put together with the involvement of the imagination, the mind and the heart, with complete concentration and involvement of your thoughts and your being, to accomplish what is to be done to the best of your capacity. The material or the objects put together will come to a complete balance. Harmony and unity become part of the accomplishment and it radiates harmony and peace. Tranquility becomes part of its character. And that object inspires a deeper thought. That object becomes connected to spirit on a deeper level. It inspires higher ideas and the higher ideas become a liaison between the spirit and the world.

When you work with the material and your spirit is part of it, then the spirit within you will give life to the material that you are working with. That material becomes an object of inspiration, unlike what you see in department stores, where the object, regardless of its shining embellishments, looks so meaningless, so worthless and so dead. The material found in a pyramid of people who died thousands of years ago is more alive than the material made by people who are supposed to be alive now. This material is made by the people who are alive, but the material is dead, because those live people have dead spirits.

Wherever you turn, you see spiritless people with the mentality of chickens, who have lost their peace of mind and can't sleep because a coyote rented a small studio apartment next to the chicken coop. Unless those spiritless people get the spirit, they will stay spiritless. And the coyote will be sitting in front of his apartment, ready to hunt them.

They seek happiness and contentment, running in all directions to catch that happiness and contentment. Happiness and contentment run away from them. True happiness and contentment never feel happy or content with the spiritless man. True happiness and contentment only find home in a heart that is pure and in a mind without polluted thoughts.

When a man has no spirit and he doesn't know how to find spirit, he settles for phony and unreal happiness and contentment, assuming the unreal is real. And if he doesn't know the real, the unreal to him is real. A duck will never know the depth of the sea. And a man without spirit will never know the depth of life, the charm, the beauty, the magic and the love that make life more alive, more tender, more sweet and more a joy and delight. But a man without spirit will settle for his happiness and contentment in a bar, for beer and a topless dancer and he thinks he is in heaven.

When a human being uses his intellect, there is no intelligence of the heart. The nature of his intellect will be doubt and suspicion. But if there is intelligence in the heart, the intellect will be like a sailboat on a smooth sea. Without the intelligence of the heart, the human being will be lost in a maze of wrong and confused thoughts. He will be lost in bars, malls, department stores, offices, factories, highways and so on. He keeps producing goods without knowing when to stop.

He thinks if he stops, he is halting the march of civilization and the march of nickels and dimes. But the production becomes more than what he needs. In that state, the production becomes worthless junk and trash. And the march of civilization becomes the march of junk and trash.

When the junk and trash can't move, it becomes a useless burden or lost matter that is cut from its origin and has lost its connection to its source and becomes a waste and an act of plundering the planet. It becomes a burden on the spirit, that is, if that person has spirit.

If he has no spirit, he will be in the same predicament as the lost matter, because matter cannot think. That person cannot think straight. If he does think straight, he will not be lost. He will know how to put the matter in its proper place and to be the master of the matter and not have the matter enslave him and cause his mind to be warped and keep him running on the highway for the sake of the matter, whether in the shape of cufflinks or an exclusive painting frame that overwhelms the painting and becomes a barrier to reduce and abuse the painting itself.

A person only needs one cup to be used for coffee and maybe a few more for guests and friends. The cup he has will last him all his life unless the cup breaks. By then he could get another one. A person does not need 1,000 cups. One cup is sufficient and that cup has value for him. All that he needs is one cup instead of 1,000. The other 999 cups are of no value to him. To store them in his house or garage will only be a sheer act of stupidity. And this could only be performed by a person without spirit.

ଚ୍ଚ

Nature abolishes and destroys, in time, anything that does not coincide with nature and is not part of the creation as a whole.

Two Weeks Vacation and Comments of Sami Ali

The man who gets angry is incapable of introspection. If he were capable of introspection, he would not be angry. An angry man is positively stupid. A man who is swallowed by the trivial, materialistic system is also incapable of introspection. Otherwise, he will not be swallowed by the trivial, materialistic system. His mind is shrivelled because he deals with all kinds of situations in the fake and phony reality of material that contributes to the elimination of the true intelligence of the heart and keeps him swinging on a thin string that connects to the shallow intellect which operates from the head.

Anxiety, the shallow intellect of the head, and abuse of material are the culprits that destroy the spirit in a man and make him a victim of his lower desires. His animal self becomes vicious with greed. He develops a lust for everything. He becomes like a frog who runs after a fly and on the edge of a well, jumps to catch the fly. He falls in a deep, dark, waterless well where he cannot see the light. It is the same with the materialistic man, as if he is in a deep dark well and cannot see the light, nor distinguish between light and dark.

Have you ever seen a cow that eats all day and all night without knowing the differences between day or night? Chewing grass does not require a chandelier. But the cow has no telephone to call the electric man to come and install the chandelier.

Materialistic man is no more than a chicken without its head, running down the highway. If the materialistic man has intelligence of the heart, he will stop driving his car immediately and question himself. "What am I doing?" and "What is it all about?" and "Why am I spending half my life driving in a hurry and working all year in an office with two weeks vacation? What kind of life is that? Even a donkey does not work all year and I only have two weeks vacation!"

"I have been working year in and year out to seek health and wealth for the sake of chattel, but for all of that I get perturbation. Besides, I neither have health nor wealth. I drive an extra eight hours a week to see a psychologist to find out what is wrong with me. I have been doing this for seven years and I still cannot find out what is wrong with me. All that I have gotten from this psychologist is to tell me to 'Look for the light at the end of the tunnel.' But the tunnel could be so long that I will forget what I'm looking for. Then the psychologist said, 'Keep grinding meat and eat hamburger, then you will be able to run faster toward the light at the end of the tunnel.'"

He said that he lived in the Middle East and learned there how to transform flat tasteless hamburger into excellent shish kebab. That is by mixing lean ground meat with chopped onion and parsley, and adding pinenuts, black pepper, curry, basil and salt, then flattening into patties before putting them in the broiler. When they are cooked, you eat them with basmati rice. They are delicious and will take you away from your perturbation, especially if you have with them a special salad made of red, ripe, organic tomatoes with green pepper, onion, cucumbers and celery, all chopped finely and dressed with cold pressed olive oil and lemon, sprinkled with chopped mint, basil, dill and parsley, with salt and black pepper added to it. And aged garlic pickles accentuate the taste, the pleasure, the delight and put you in a state of elation and euphoria and bring you to a contentment and joy that has never existed in a hot dog or hamburger.

There are all the chances in the world that you will not only forget the light at the end of the tunnel, but you will also forget who you are. You will forget that you are a materialistic machine. You will forget all the stupid things that you have been doing all your life, that get you nothing but aggravation and complication and only sweat and toil. And, at the end of your life, you come out as a flat-dimensional human being without wisdom or knowledge. And what could be expected when you were a machine all your life? A machine at the end of its life becomes a broken machine.

When I was in the Middle East, I visited Egypt, the Sudan, Jordan, Lebanon, Syria, Iraq, Saudi Arabia and Yemen. In all of these countries, I never saw a single man or woman as a machine. They all seemed extremely friendly, happy and generous, with shining eyes and radiant smiles. A six-year-old child there has more understanding and wisdom than many rigid and stiff-faced professors.

I asked one Egyptian, "You must have a lot of excellent psychologists to have this great ease and joy in life!"

Sami Ali, the Egyptian replied, "What is that?! What is the meaning of psychologist?"

I told him that a psychologist is a specialist in changing the sickness of the mind in people when they have trouble, anger and confusion, and in bringing them back to normal.

Sami Ali said, "We don't have any of these problems. These are the work of the devil. When people have no faith in themselves and the reality and the life, they fall easy prey to the devil. He controls them, abuses them, makes them do all the wrong things and makes them incapable of distinguishing between wrong and right. They become lustful and greedy and have low desires. These things will destroy the righteousness, the magnanimity and the wisdom. The people will run in all directions, without knowing what they are doing. They destroy their health with food that is filled with poison. Under these conditions, no one is safe from this tribulation. They are trapped and there is no way out. Fear and anxiety fill all the cells in their body.

"The collective result of this will be collective anxiety and fear in the identity of man. He projects anxiety and fear on to anything that he comes in contact with. Anxiety and fear become more natural than the real nature of man. He no longer knows any better, because he is in a society where everyone is a victim of these diseases of the mind. When men like him gather together, they will have tension and fear shooting out and circulating like fireworks in one of the evening celebrations in Disneyland.

"I know all of that and more, because I have visited these so-called technical, industrial and civilized western nations. I went to seek enlightenment from these great civilizations. But I found people that had lost their connection to humanity. In fact, they were too far gone to describe them as people with gentle manners. They did not react like human beings. Compassion and love did not exist. They could not relate to each other. They did not have creative minds and they had no words to say to each other. The joy, man to man, in conversation, did not exist. The majority of them had sullen faces, because the vital energy had been depleted from their anxiety and negative thinking about taxes, bills and the expense of repairing their cars or losing their jobs."

"Many mothers tell their children, 'Don't talk to strangers!'"

"And the child says, 'Why?!'"

"The mother will say, 'He will make you a barbecue and eat you and then you cannot eat Twinkies.'"

"And the child says, 'But Mommy, the man asked me if I wanted a Twinkie.'"

"But the mother said, 'No, Tommy, don't do that. The Twinkie he has contains a scorpion. It will bite you on the tongue and you cannot eat anymore. The Twinkie I have has chocolate and cream filling.'"

Sami Ali said, "This is what I meant by too far gone. In this society, what they need is a complete overhaul, a clearance as human beings. They should forget the clearance in their department stores. The real clearance that they need is in their minds, in their psyches, in their spirits, in their bodies, in their imaginations, in their well being, in their wisdom, in their understanding and in their relations with each other, to free themselves from the slavery of materialistic ignorance and useless lust and to become human beings again."

The Koran says plainly, "A slave mind is incapable of doing anything good and great."

And the Koran also points out, "Man's dealings with man may be a source of bliss and comfort."

૪૭

If the life uses you, your life will shrink. If you use the life, your life will expand.

When the Time
Eats Man Alive

When a man strangles his spirit by his own doing, the depth of his essence disappears. Then a gaudy embellishment becomes the cover of his distortion. The destruction and gratification of his self snatches him out of the existence of peace and into the existence of trial and tribulation.

He will suffer, because he puts too much importance and greatness on things that are not so important or great. Actually, they are vain things and a complete waste of energy, vitality, strength, tranquility, peace, humanity and intelligence.

In a materialistic society, man is born heedless of the spirit and of the true and beautiful reality of which he knows nothing. He plays with toys and finishes his life playing with toys. He leaves this life as he came, except that he leaves it with misery, confusion, ignorance and without knowing the meaning of life or what the purpose of existence is, because he has wasted his existence in a life that is useless and gloomy, seeking nothing but gratification of the self and the senses, and being more and more greedy and selfish.

Selfishness and greed are the fuel for anxiety, tension and confusion, and reduce a man to the lowest existence. A human being goes far away from anything that could be called a human being. He becomes a creature, neither human nor animal, neither dead nor alive. For him, nobility is a word that has no meaning and is coming from the last planet in the galaxy on its way to the last planet on the other side of the galaxy.

The man goes through his life to the end pursuing a counterfeit reality. Then, the stiff mask he wears on his face becomes permanent when the brain becomes a paradoxical arena of conflict, contention and combat.

Spiritless people rejoice in their own destruction, believing that they are having a great time. But the great time will eat them alive. One morning, they will wake up and find that the life has gone, just as if it had never existed. What will remain is a faint picture with dim images, distorted forms, weak remembrance and sad sentimentality for something that has finished and gone.

The joy that was, the fun, the play, the restaurants, the fancy dinners and the lust for more and more of everything and anything, all come to an end when the body and the will lose their capacity, flexibility and exuberance, as old age grips them and they stoop from it.

It is just like a lush, lovely and beautiful green meadow that is invaded by a million grasshoppers. In no time, all that lush, lovely, beautiful meadow disappears, as if it had never existed and gloom and despair is what is left. That is exactly what is waiting for heedless and careless human beings. Gloom and despair will fill them wherever they are or wherever they go.

For people who live for their senses and pleasure, it is not possible to comprehend the splendor and magnificence of the true pleasure of the spirit. It is too late to do anything about it now, but never too late to learn. At least one thing presents itself in practicality and that is not to be sorry or sad for what is gone or has slipped away from your hands. To be sorry or not sorry gets you nowhere when you are at the end of the line. So get your alignment balanced and plunge forth to wherever you're going, with a bottle of wine to ease your expectation and numb you before you get in the complete numbness.

Flat Man

When a tire has no air you call it flat. So when a man has no spirit you could call him a flat man. He is equal to a flat tire. In a society that doesn't know anything about the spirit, wherever you go you see nothing but flat tires, whether in a mall, in a shop, in a grocery, on the street or on the beach.

A tire performs at its best when the air is in it and a man functions at his best when the spirit is in him. A tire without air becomes rubber. A man without spirit becomes merely a form.

৪৩গ৪

Don't expect a lush green garden when there is no rain or water. And don't expect wisdom if you are stupid.

Basement Apartment

The moment is the corridor that opens on eternity. When you are not in the moment, it is like being in a basement – dark, dingy, cold and humid, with a leak and a thousand roaches and a dirty carpet that smells like a dead mouse. And actually, there is a dead mouse under it. That basement is in New York where the rent is $750, because it is in an excellent location and you don't have to take the subway. It is near many bars. It is also next to a German cake and pastry shop where the chocolate cake is divine. Next to the German pastry shop is a Korean Green Grocer. Next to that is a 31 Flavors ice cream shop. Across the street is a movie theater that is open all night, specializing in foreign films and tantric sensual and spiritual films.

If it happens that you get in the moment, it is as if you are suddenly transported to a tropical island with lovable sunsets and pure, clean air that is carried on wave after wave from beyond the horizon, and organic baby bananas ripe, tender and sweet. They taste as if they are stuffed with wild honey from the Manzano Mountains and mango and papaya to accentuate the pleasure of the taste. And if you taste, you will know and if you don't taste, you will never know.

To taste the life in that dark, dingy basement is unlike the taste of the sunset, the pure air, the dancing waves and the baby sweet bananas. Take your pick. If you know how to get in the moment, the moment will lead you to paradise.

ಸೂಲ

The Blessing

When you have spirit and you do anything with material, technology, thought or deed, the spirit within you permeates the object that you are working with or the thought or the deed and they become spiritualized.

The object or the material that you are working with will have a feeling of contentment and refinement. The thought that has spirit radiates a pleasant flow. The thought that has spirit has continuous sweet remembrance.

Baraka, blessing, comes from the spirit. *Baraka* is the nature of spirit. It is a positive force that burns the negative force in its presence. *Baraka* purifies the heart, the body, the mind, the psyche and the emotions. *Baraka* makes life beautiful. *Baraka* give you charm and makes you congenial. *Baraka* makes the surroundings and nature appealing. Your life becomes delightful and you give delight.

The pleasure of *baraka* is a unique state which cannot be compared or comprehended. It is unknown to people who are not in contact with *baraka*. It is tender, soft and pure contentment which comes not from doing or accomplishing something. It is a contentment that comes from a heavenly source. It is a gift that transcends and surpasses any gain on the material level. It comes when you are ready, when the heart is pure and receptive.

Baraka is made of the extract of existence. It is the cream of creation, the delight of heaven. *Baraka* is in the blue color of the sky. *Baraka* is in the pure rain. *Baraka* is in the vivacious and playful clouds. *Baraka* is in the lavish, tender breath of life. *Baraka* is in the smile of the eyes when the eyes are filled with spirit. *Baraka* is in the vision when the vision sees the spirit. *Baraka* is in the heart when the heart dances with the spirit. *Baraka* is when your heart is open to that tremendous force and power of pure love that is waiting outside of you in the space.

Baraka will put you on smooth waves in a sailboat on the sea of life and existence. *Baraka* is in the heart of the people of spirit. *Baraka* is in the love when love comes from spirit. *Baraka* is when the love is beautiful. *Baraka* is when the love is life and life is love. *Baraka* is when love and life flow into each other.

Baraka is the depth of heaven. *Baraka* is the beauty of the stars and the light of the moon. *Baraka* is the breeze and the dancing clouds in the playfulness of winds. *Baraka* is the colorful sunset in its reflection on the quivering waves.

ଅଠ

When you have spirit, you become a friend of God. God said in the Koran, "The friends of God, no fear or sorrow will fall on them."

The Duck that Swims in Boiling Oil

If you know then you will have understanding. If you don't know, then you will not have understanding. If you don't know and you want to know from the one who knows, then you will know. If you don't know and you don't want to know, then you will not know.

When the spirit is alive, the mind becomes still and the words become a sweet vehicle for spirit. Harmony and peace come with them. But when the mind is negative, the words will vibrate with quivering tension and fear. It is like putting a duck to swim in boiling oil. God created the duck to swim in cool water, not in boiling oil. And God created people to flow in harmony in the life and not to make the life disastrous and confused.

God said in the Koran, "God wills your comfort not your discomfort."

When the mind is still, you will learn natural wisdom, not from a book of paper, but from the book of nature. The book of nature is the environment, time, space and the world that is around you. Natural wisdom is a truthful experience when it is positive. It will bring peace, harmony and life. Life becomes meaningful. The heart opens with the spirit and is filled with contentment in the moment. The moment dances with the moment and they spill their pleasure onto each other. The time and space hug each other with joy. The environment becomes harmonious and the countenance of the environment smiles at you and spills the pleasure of the two moments onto your heart. Love sprouts in the soul and makes your heart fly with a song of delight.

When the positive essence within you opens, it will join the positive essence of existence that makes you feel as if you are in heaven. But when your thought is negative, your heart becomes black and your mind becomes the mind of a mule. Your spirit disappears and the moment becomes agonizing, torturous and unbearable. It is as if you have fallen into a dark deep pit filled with poisonous snakes that have a fearful hate of man. It is for you to imagine what will take place in that dark deep pit of misery and death.

People without spirit who talk, shout and scream for peace in the world, whether on radio, television, in the newspaper or in conversation, will never have it, even if they could achieve peace among men by not killing each other and not going to war. The real peace is actually when you are at peace with yourself. This peace is hard to get because it is not a commodity to be bought in a glittering, fancy department store.

These department stores are only graveyards where people go and bury their spirit, then seek consolation in all kinds of food, desserts and ice creams, foods that make people sick. When food has no nutrition and no taste, it will bring no contentment or satisfaction. People keep eating and eating without getting satisfied. They get fatter and fatter and there is no limit to how fat they get because there is no limit to how unsatisfactory the food is.

It is greed and selfishness that creates all kinds of junky, poisonous, unhealthy food to feed the people, because those makers of food have no spirit. They don't have appreciation or understanding for either food or people. They, themselves, are poisoned with their own poison. There is a gloomy dark cloud that keeps tension and anxiety over those people. Complaining is their favorite pastime. And complaining is disrespectful and a profanity to God.

God said in the Koran, "If you speak and say sweet words, they will go to heaven and come down as blessings."

It is truly very easy to get blessings if you try to be nice and say pleasant things to your friends, to people, to animals or to anyone. Life becomes sweet and pleasant with sweet and pleasant words.

I have observed that people who are negative and complaining constantly get into a worse and worse state of confusion, misery and ugliness. They vibrate energy that would terrify even a decent devil.

From what I have read in the Koran, "Sweet words go to heaven and come down as blessings," I made my own hypothesis. According to my own observation of negative and complaining people, complaining words go to the hellfire, that you read about in the Bible, and come back to you as horror, panic and damnation.

The only way to save yourself from the most miserable situation in the entire world, and the darkness and misery of the world, is to go to the spirit, to be pure, to clean yourself from filth and to be generous and beautiful. There is nothing easier than saying sweet words. Keep saying sweet words and you will be sweet. It is an easy and simple way. Try it and you will lose nothing and you will gain everything.

If you insist on being negative and complaining, then you have no intelligence. Stupidity, negativity and complaining are all in the same family. So, if you can't say sweet words, watch the TV show "All in the Family" with Archie Bunker and Edith. Have a beer with beer nuts, have a laugh, drink a lot, a lot of beer and then go to your bed and have a heavy, thick sleep.

In the morning, complain to your boss on the telephone saying, "I have a headache. I'm dizzy and I can't come to the office. If you please, call Kelly Girl to work for me and handle all the papers on my desk. I really wanted to come and I took a dozen aspirin but when I stood up to brush my teeth, I felt dizzy and drowsy. I looked in the mirror and saw my face was yellow and gray. My nose twitched and my cheeks quivered and my teeth were going click, click, click without me saying a word. I was terrified and I started involuntarily screaming and shouting."

"I heard the neighbors' little boy shouting to his father, 'Daddy, Daddy, there is a donkey in the neighbor's bathroom hee hawing. Go get him out. I want to ride him.'"

"And the father said, 'Be quiet, Georgie. There is no donkey in the bathroom. It sounds more like a monkey. I heard the neighbor yesterday talking about buying a monkey.'"

৪০ ৫৪

Any action that does not lead to the development of being and spirit is a lost action.

63

China Doll

God lives in the moment and if you get in the moment, you will be with God. And the moment is the house of God. And He will give you cosmic candy unknown to human beings.

You live in the moment every moment of your life, but you never know the moment and its charm, tranquility, peace, beauty and magic because you think of the past. You become scatterbrained and the moment does not appear to scattered people. The moment rejects anything that does not coincide with it in peace, tranquility and intelligence. The moment does not recognize the past or the future.

Past or future only exist in the intellect of the head when the spirit is dead. When the spirit is dead, you will not have the intelligence of the heart. It will be utterly impossible to be in the moment. The moment is the link between earth and heaven. And when you are in it, tranquility, peace, mercy and healing descend to your heart from heaven.

For millions and millions of people, to get in the moment does not exist and is unknown. The closest they come to the moment is when they say, "Give me a moment, I'm coming." Then, the other person will say, "You said 'Give me a moment, I'm coming,' but I've already waited ten minutes and I'm getting nervous and tense."

I could say all the people in the materialistic and technological societies who look to material as the charm of life think they are snake charmers. But the snake that they charm is a plastic snake. They are born and go through life looking for happiness, contentment and pleasure but they cannot find it. And the most amazing thing is that they are existing in the moment and in the life, but they never know the moment.

Their life has been completely empty as if they had never lived regardless of their accomplishments, even if they believe that their accomplishments had a beneficial effect on humanity and the world and made a great episode in the history. But those people don't know who they are and have never even dreamt about the present, even in their sleep.

When the spirit does not exist, the present becomes a plastic doll from Hong Kong. So, for those people, the best thing to do is to study Chinese. And maybe that will lead them to learn about Confucius, to get them out of their misery and confusion. Maybe by then, they will be in the image of God and not in the image of a wino on the Bowery or in a celebrated grand ball room in any of the grand hotels. And if you do not have a knack for Confucianism, eat Chinese food and ask for a fortune cookie and say "Hallelujah."

ଡ଼ଔ

A balance between material and spirit will bring a happy, ideal life to humanity.

The Brook, the Daffodil, Contentment and the Nightingale

When you are not centered, irritation becomes your inclination. And when the mind and heart are covered with darkness, you will see the world in darkness. Your eyes look gloomy and your voice quivers. You experience the hell in this world before finding if there is hell later on and you never know what contentment is. Without contentment, you will never know the meaning of life and the joy of living.

Contentment is the inner secret of life that is hidden in the heart. When the heart opens, contentment will become part of you. And each moment of contentment is filled with the nectar of paradise.

To get contentment, you need to have a good relationship with your spirit. The spirit is the living love when you live it. Contentment is its simple and easy product, just like the flow of pure water in a beautiful brook that is surrounded by tender, sweet, smiling daffodils, with charming songs of sparrows, birds and nightingales.

Every man could be in a similar state or situation if he wished. But the secret is how to pamper your heart and how to soothe your mind. It is as easy as the murmuring, pure water in the brook, with the daffodils and singing birds. If you know how to access the intelligence of the heart and not the intellect in your head, you will get the best. If you go to the intellect of the head, you will learn to work with tools, machines, computers, office work and tons of papers, so much so, that your face will look like white paper. All of these things are children's play, except that children would get bored with it and leave it, even if the world came to a stop. To children, it doesn't matter whether the world stops or runs fast. It is all the same and it all comes out in the wash.

All of what people like to do is secondary or relative. If they put all the importance on the relative, they will never find the real. It is only in the real that a man can ascend to the height of vision, awareness and knowledge of the self and the cosmos. Both the knowledge of the self and cosmos will bring tranquility, contentment, peace and evolution which bring perfection to man. Then, you could say man is created in the image of God. Anything short of that and you could say, man is created in the image of an ignorant, silly and heedless creature.

Mohammed said, "People are either possessors of inner knowledge or seekers of that knowledge. And there is nothing good outside of that."

80CB

Use the life before the life uses you. When the life uses you, you are finished and that is the end of it.

Infinite Lust, the Sergeant and the Cat

Thought is complete freedom when it is pure and truthful and it is anxiety and tension when it is polluted. Confusion is unknown to it when a man is in contact with his spirit.

Bigotry is a reflection of ignorance and anger is its product. When a man is angry, he represents stupidity. A foolish man has a monopoly on his foolishness, afraid of others transgressing on his grandiose feat.

Spiritualism is dead in the heart of materialistic people. They can't say the word spirit, because fear and horror grab at their necks. The devil chokes their throat to keep them away from the spirit, even if it is in the form of a word.

The identity of materialism is made up of cardboard just like a cardboard house. When the rain comes and the storms blow, it will crumble, just like the crumbs of rice cake and fall apart like a little paper child made boat that melts in the lake.

Chocolate mousse has a strong foundation and is even heavy to look at. A dog will eat a chocolate mousse cake with a quivering shake from the excitement of encountering chocolate mousse cake for the first time in his life. And if the dog wants to be spiritual, he's got to start somewhere. That dog, if he encounters a rice cake, will not sniff it with the tip of his nose. And you cannot blame a dog for his delight in a gourmet dessert.

The universe has no end. It is infinite. A man and a dog are inside of it. They cannot be on the outside, because no one knows the outside, neither the man nor the dog. But the man is given intelligence which is as precious and as important as the universe itself. If the man is not given that intelligence, his worth will be as important as the intelligence of a grasshopper. Then, the dog will have the upper hand regarding the man.

So what will it be? To be or not to be? To be Mr. Grasshopper or Mr. Man? So, this Mr. Man, if he doesn't wake up from his trivial life style of lust and greed, if he doesn't wake up, surely he will be Mr. Grasshopper, hoarding and gathering whatever his hands can get hold of.

What a strange, baffling situation for a man to milk the cow until the blood comes out, with his scientific, technological gadget that puts the cow in a state of shock.

God said in the Koran, "I give you everything that you desire and if you count the blessings of God you will have no number to contain them." God said, "I give you the world and whatever in it, I give you the sun, the moon, the air, the water, the land and the seas." Man turns around and destroys this magical world. This is truly the work of a man that is possessed by the devil.

The greed of the materialistic people is infinite. The spirit is dead in their hearts and the devil will take its place. They want to eat anything that their eyes see and drink anything that comes in bottles. They would not hesitate to drink all the water in the seas, if the seas had no salt. There is no doubt at all that if a notion came to their conspiring minds to put sugar in black oil and drink it as a tonic, they would gladly do so on the pretext that God gave them a mouth to be practical. If the mouth is there, then why not use it? Sweet black oil is better than bitter. The sweetness of the oil has an appeal to the tastebuds of the lustful, hedonist, materialistic people, who are, in reality, ignorant of the real taste of anything that has a taste.

When spirit does not exist, whatever the materialistic people do will have no taste. Without spirit, a man is an animal, no better than a cat or a dog. In fact, the cat and dog are better than him, because they are natural, have good intentions, and follow the creed of *fitra*, which means the natural way created without complication.

Man lost the *fitra* by creating many twists in his mind that drive him far away and put him in the darkest reality, so that the nature, reality and existence flee from him, as a bird flees from the vicinity of starving, hungry, acrobatic cats, that jump, twist and do somersaults in the air for the floating, soft, fuzzy feather of a bird.

Incidentally, that cat saw a floating feather and smelled the taste of a bird in it and quicker than lightening jumped in the air ten feet high, twisted and did a somersault and dove at the feather like an arrow let fly from the hand of magnificent Chief Red Cloud. That arrow penetrated the nose of Sergeant Red Chuck and went through his nose so that he never even felt a pinch, because of the intense speed of the arrow.

Later on in his tent, he felt an itch in his nose. He had a piece of broken mirror and he looked in it and saw a hole in his nose. He jumped up, proclaiming with a high voice, "Holy jackrabbit, God must want me to have a hole in my nose. I will wear a turquoise colored ring in my nose. I have found some crystals and they give me high energy. And, right in the moment, I will be a New Age healer. My name is Red and for the New Age, I will change it to Red River.

Back to the cat — that cat dove at the feather like an arrow with his mouth wide open. The cat quickly closed his mouth to catch the feather, but with a little miscalculation. Actually, there were two feathers and the cat didn't know which to catch. They were bulky feathers and each feather went far into each nostril of the cat. The cat fell down breathless, sneezing, because the feather tickled the cat deep in the nose. The cat started laughing hysterically and the feathers would not come out. And this is the fate of the materialistic people. They get stuck with the material, just like the cat is stuck with the feathers. It tickles them and they suffer from the intensity of the tickle and they eat more pickle.

The materialistic people get stuck with the material in their spirit and they don't know what to do about it. It is like a person in a backward, foreign country where the water is polluted. If he drinks it, he will die. And the temperature is 120 degrees. It is hot, hot, hot, dry, dry, dry. And the person becomes extremely, violently thirsty and there is nothing to drink but cola. He drinks cola, but it does not quench the thirst for water, especially after having a dinner at noontime with hot spice and pickle with vinegar made from dates in Baghdad and that is the best, strongest and tangiest vinegar in the world. If you are in a moderate, benign climate and you drink a teaspoon of it, that tangy taste will make you do the tango on the spot.

The materialistic people and the material they possess are possessed by each other. They seek happiness and contentment from the material, but what happens is that the material and their indulgence in it, without understanding, brings them weakness, sickness, anxiety, tension and limitless problems. The crux of the matter is how to get out of that situation when there is no sight of a solution for the predicament they are in. This is attributable to the absence of spirit and lacking the understanding to bring the situation to a decent, honorable, balanced state of life.

The solution is to go back to humanity, the natural humanity that is connected with the love of heart and not the rag tag humanity that has lost faith in human beings. These human beings have become useless auxiliary parts of machines, computers and offices, that breed sterilization in human character and dignity and make the people zombies, incapable of any perceptions outside of their dull screens of drafting and calculation. All the things they eat cause them to be weak, sick and filled with anxiety and fear. They accumulate heaps of fat on their bodies which you could call "office fat." And they are already stiff beyond flexibility.

It would be better for those people to watch and learn from a cat or dog, preferably to watch the cat and dog in the country in their natural habitat and to be free from hepatitis. All cats and dogs who live in cities with their masters develop the same personality, traits and characteristics as their masters. So, they are not normal or natural and malnutrition causes them to be unbalanced. Giving a dog dog-cookies is not natural for the dog. You do it because of affection for the dog, but in the long run the dog will suffer from sickness and disease, just like his master.

To watch normal, natural cats and dogs, you will learn about *fitra*, which is a beautiful, natural state of existence.

Serenity is their disposition. When the dog barks, it is a recognition of the magic of voice that is created in him. When the cat meows, it is a voice of life and a voice in life that assures life. Life with voice is the spice of life and a sign pointing to the reality and connection to the truth. A dog will never hesitate to bark. It makes him feel good, energized.

But many men are frightened to talk and the words melt and disappear before they come out of the mouth. Their tongues are twisted and the mouth of material, in Arabic, *Al Aeth*, eats their spirit. Besides, no one is receptive to what they will say. It is positively not in the nature of materialistic people to say anything of interest. Their conversation is dead and plastic. The intelligence of the materialistic man, who has intelligence but no spirit, becomes corroded and limited. He is confused, because he does things that are against nature and against his nature. Spiritlessness and unnaturalness in man will produce corrupted material and strife. But when spirit and your own nature combine, they will produce spiritualized material and felicity.

The man who spends all of his life working day in and day out until he dies is a lost man. It doesn't matter how much he accomplishes in material, it will do him no good; all is a waste of time. It doesn't matter how much he accomplishes in material, he is an ignorant man. He doesn't know who he is and what life is about. He never reflects on one moment in his life or on the spirit, because he thinks no such thing exists. His brain crumbles like an iron bridge hit by a bomb. His face is twisted with a monkey wrench, so that his face looks like a monkey, but without the pleasure that you see on the face of a real monkey. It will be like a universal phenomenon to make that man smile.

In materialistic societies, people eat poison, drink poison and breathe poison that causes fusion in the cells of the face, as if you had been welding them with a torch. That is the reason why materialistic man can't smile. It is a horrendous act of violence against the fused cells in the face of the man.

The Woody People

The spirit of materialistic people is made of wood. And some of them wear a stuffed, stiff shirt to appease and please the stiff, woody spirit within themselves when they go ballroom dancing. Woody spirited people in materialistic society have stiff, twisted faces. A smile is not in their nature. Anxiety and fear fill their hearts.

They don't talk to each other, whether in a train, a plane or a bus or in the streets. Each one looks at the others as if they were cannibals and could jump at him anytime to eat him. And they take advantage of malls and department stores to wear clothes to pretend that they are civilized. It is a camouflage and a setup for a new hunt. Woody the Woodpecker has more fun in life, because his heart is made of love, songs and laughter.

৪৩୪৪

If you are truthful to finding the spirit, the spirit will smile on you and take you by the hand and show you a garden the likes of which you have never seen in all your life.

Society of Tension

The more you control the negative self, the more understanding grows in the positive self. A natural merriment flourishes in the soul. The soul becomes happy and appreciates action in the right direction and a natural merriment paves the way to a beautiful and sweet knowledge of the heart. This knowledge is based on and immersed in the consciousness within, which is connected to the cosmic consciousness.

It is more delightful to be near a beautiful murmuring stream which fills the heart with happiness than to be near a murmuring, gloomy, sullen-faced man who fills the atmosphere with miserable ugliness while complaining about the hot dog shop where he has to eat his hot dog without mustard because they were out of it. And the soft drink was hot, the coffee was cold, and the apple turnover was sour.

He says, "I will never ever go to this hot dog shop again, even if they give me a bucket of mustard and all the apple turnovers in the world. I feel hurt and my nerves start tingling. I feel jittery and my ulcers start erupting in pain. My cheeks start to twitch and my constitutional right is violated."

A dog is a million times better than a self-centered man whose animal soul controls him and whose spirit is dead. A man like that is not fit to be with human beings or even with animals, because animals never complain. And if they find mustard they will say, "Oh good, we will have it with the grass and call it garden green salad. And if there is no mustard, it will be just the same and we will call it a strict, macrobiotic, green grass, delicious dinner."

A man without spirit is the worst creature on the face of the earth. He is the product of a materialistic society that finds pleasure in a plastic duck. There are many of these men and their number is on the rise in the materialistic society. That is a society of neither animals nor of human beings, a society that is filled with tension, misery, violence and crime, a sick society that can't cure itself because the cure does not exist.

When the spirit is dead, there is nothing on earth to cure a man. He will be a replica of a man put together by selfishness, greed, desires, headlessness, habits, liquor, drugs, chemical food, physical, mental and psychic disturbance and a dead intellectualism and plastic mentality with the smile of a frozen cabbage. He will be a junky man who lives in stress and struggle and never knows what is the meaning of a man. He will die and never use his faculties in a positive direction, but always in a negative way. But he is given faculties that are very capable of discovering and finding marvels, charm and magic.

People in a materialistic society have apprehension and fear about the word "spirit." When you don't know something, you will fear it, even if it is good for you.

A proverb in the Middle East goes, "The evil that you know is better than the good that you don't know."

For instance, if people never know anything about cake, they will only know that there is something called cake. But if they have never seen or known anything about cake, they will develop apprehension about it and what it really is. And they will have suspicion and fear.

Possibly they might think the cake is a monstrous creature which might come and eat them. Wouldn't that be great, if people were afraid of cake? Then they would lose weight and look healthy with shining eyes and radiant smiles. They might even look like the Bedouins in the desert who never having had cake in their lives, are firm, trim, and peaceful. If they ever did taste it, they would spit it out, saying, "Impure weak food makes people weak. Weak people are burdens on the spirit."

So, it is the same with the spirit, especially when someone among them filibusters the people about spirit, claiming expertise and mastery of the spirit. He culminates his wisdom, knowledge and command of the spirit by telling the people, "If you don't have spirit, you will be put in hellfire."

But this wise man who knows all about spirit evidently could not tell them how to get the spirit. Spirit is not a commodity that can be attained in the grocery. There is nothing worse than a man who is ignorant, but thinks he knows.

Mohammed said, "There are four kinds of men. The first is a man who knows and he knows that he knows; he is a learned man, learn from him. The second is a man who knows and he doesn't know that he knows; he is forgetful, remind him. The third man doesn't know and he knows that he doesn't know; he is a seeker, teach him. And the fourth man doesn't know and he doesn't know that he doesn't know; he is stupid, stay away from him."

The man who tries to explain spirit through the intellect of the head expounds only what is fit for fairy tales. Spirit is life, love and keenness in the intelligence of the heart. Action and experience are its realm and arena of pleasure and delight. As for ignorant people who are stuck in their head, the best thing to do is to play the tambourine, dance and sing, to get in touch with their vibration and to raise their level of energy.

God said in the Koran, "Whatever you do you will be rewarded according to your sincerity."

When spirituality is only in the head and not in the heart, the people become phony and think that they are advanced and highly developed in their accomplishments. Their bias exposes their ignorance, even if they think that they are philosophers. When people are in their heads and do a lot of reading and only stay on the level of intellect, they will have some amount of confusion because ideas, thought and hypothesis counteract each other. Sometimes there is hesitation, conflict or unsureness and many other ways and complications that are depleting to the energy and vitality, and stunt innovation and creativity. People will talk very expertly about what they have read and learned, but that is as far as it goes. The knowledge that they have is trapped and imprisoned without freedom to move. It has lost its freshness, liveliness and the beautiful challenge in it.

A book has no value unless you put what is in it into action and practice. Intellectualism without experience is like a fish out of water. The fish looks like a fish, but the fish is dead.

Intellectual knowledge, when not put into practice, will lose its meaning. It has no warmth, sincerity, life, challenge or beauty, while the intelligence that comes from the heart has useful meaning. It has warmth that makes the environment cozy. It has sincerity that gives you peace. It has life that animates the roses with perfume from heaven. It has a challenge and no other challenge comes close or near to it. It is a superior knowledge that is inspired by the spirit. It fills your heart, your being, the existence and the cosmos with life, love, contentment, evolution, innovation, higher intelligence, higher perceptions and dynamic humanism, and it creates unity with the elements, with life and love, the creation and with heaven. It is *Al Tawhid*, unity with no separation, unity with strength and power. Separation is weakness and disintegration. It is all up to you to be strong or weak. Pick what you like. If you want to rise to levels that lift you to the utmost fulfillment in life, do something about it. Otherwise, you will stay in the compartment of the weak and the confused.

৪৩৪৪

The pleasures of the senses are passing pleasures that leave you empty, dreary, sorrowful and sentimental. They are the product of a fleeting moment.

Beauty Parlor
and the Creation

However your thought will be, you will be. A good thought with a good intention puts you in paradise here on earth. A bad thought with a bad intention puts you in hell here on earth. Have positive thought and your surroundings will be like a blooming rose. Have a negative thought and wherever you look will be gloomy and dark. You will be in a circle surrounded by a thousand scorpions, each of them as big as a water buffalo with their poisonous tails curved up like the Arch of Victory in Paris. These scorpions have the mind of a sinister, scheming, criminal, materialistic man. All of them want to choke you to death, because you have a jar of honey. And they think it is important and necessary to take the honey from you, to put it on hot toast with butter for breakfast.

By not stopping the thought that comes from greed, selfishness, low desire and wicked thinking, you allow yourself to be base and insignificant and to be in the lowest of the low and the darkest of the dark of existence, where misery and disaster never leave you. A choking anxiety like a vice heartedly opens, waiting to grab you, to embrace you. The two jaws of the vice will love to hold you tight and chew you relentlessly without a respite to catch your breath. It will squeeze you and tighten the hold around your neck and choke you out of your last breath. It will not kill you, but it will leave you like the walking dead.

The Koran says, "Death comes to him from every direction, but he is not dead." What God meant in the Koran by that saying was that the person who does the wrong thing will never experience harmony and peace. And I add to that, "If a person does wrong things to people and insists on doing the wrong things, without being conscientious, God will multiply his misery. The formidable ego will enjoy his suffering and blind him from seeing the right course. The ego controls the intellect and the intellect goes hodgepodge and the spirit is blind, mute and cannot hear a whisper of a bird or the sound of the vibration of a hair."

Life is not heads or tails, like flipping a coin. It is something that you form, mold, create and then set in the best of settings. Life is beautiful and life is charming when you have true love in your heart. The life worth calling life and true love cannot truly exist when you are not a true person. And there is no way in the world or in the whole existence to be a true person with vibrant love in the heart, unless you go to the spirit. All existence functions and operates through the power of spirit. The spirit exists and fills the space wherever there is space. It is in the object and the creation. But the spirit cannot be seen when the heart is made of a block of cement.

The heart that is made of a block of cement is the trademark of the people who seek comfort, happiness and utopia in material. They are unwilling to put the slightest effort to improve their humanity except bolstering and pampering the animal soul within themselves. The ego within them never knows or understands the word contentment or when enough is enough. They plunder the planet like a rabid dog who doesn't know the meaning of respect to the self, to others or to the creation. They plunder everything including their mind, their body, their soul, their personality and their own respect by being deformed human beings, through their lust for everything that they see or get hold of or anything they put in their mouths, whether hot dog, ice cream, plastic food, processed food or poisonous meat. When people are ingrained this deeply in material, they lose their sense of taste and anything they then put in their mouths they proclaim with wonder, "Oh my God, how delicious. I never had anything like that in all my life," even if they are eating the same slop everyday.

So, these people go to big grocery stores imagining they are going to a picnic outing or on a very pleasurable expedition to enjoy exploring and discovering in between the aisles, as if they are in a canyon. They look to the walls of the shelves as the most attractive mountainside. The difference is they don't climb it, but walk next to it. In these groceries, there are thousands of products. Each product there, if you taste, smell or eat it, will administer poison to your system. Those people keep eating poison and have birthday parties with cakes with all the gooey things on it and they fall in euphoria.

Year after year, you see those people declining physically, mentally, psychically and they become very receptive to sickness and diseases that never existed before in the history of humanity. They lose their connection to themselves and to other people. They cannot relate to each other. Exhaustion and tiredness permanently become part of their makeup. They smear their faces with makeup to be attractive and beautiful. But when they don't have the spirit, they could dive into a pool of multicolored paint and come out crispy colored and they will never be attractive or beautiful, because they have no spirit. The only beauty that there is, is the beauty of the spirit. Without it, you don't need to make yourself beautiful, because it will not happen. The only thing those people can achieve through a beauty parlor is facial innovation and nail manicure.

It is not a strange thing to see so many men becoming plump, with round tummies filled with all the delights they could get a hold of, whether in a restaurant, pretzel or hot dog stand, or in a grocery store. It is not becoming for a man to be like a tame rabbit, fat and clumsy, and to sit in a beauty parlor to manicure his nails. For this man, it will do him better to go and dig ditches, cut wood or run after the baby goats, to play hide and seek among the green hills and eat natural, wholesome foods from a garden of organic vegetables. Then God will bless him and give him *baraka*, respect and dignity – to be a human being with awareness, consciousness and a love in the heart big enough to be able to smile at people and to invite them to sit with him and to laugh with them with love and not to have a mechanical smile as he had at the beauty parlor.

When you work with gardens and goats, God will not only make your nails beautiful, but you will be beautiful all over. And you don't need the help of the people in the beauty parlor to make you beautiful, because they are in the same trial and tribulation as you. You both are in the same lost boat in the sea of life. If you fall from that boat of misery, you will drown in the sea of life. So, it is better to learn how to swim, because if you don't know how to swim and you fall in the sea, you will drown. Those people at the beauty parlor need to go with you to dig ditches, take care of vegetable gardens and run after the goats. Then, God will turn them into respectful human beings with dignity and spirit and they will love it. And God will love them and make them a little tribe, like the tribes in the Arabian desert. And the motto of the Arabian tribe in the desert is, "We are together and we love each other in happiness or calamity. We are one."

But the makeup and the extensive work, whether in beauty parlors or homes or the big industries that cater to making everyone beautiful, that beauty does not work. The most they can do is create images of a clumsy totem with weak imitation. I'm sure that if Red Cloud or Sitting Bull or even General Custer saw them, they would be so shocked they would run away on their horses to the Amazon jungle and form alliances of peace and never fight again, because of the horrendous shock they experienced from the totem that is produced in the beauty parlors. They will form a tribe called the tribe of NoTotem. At night, they will sit around the fire chanting, "No Totem, No Totem, God Forbid, No Totem, No Totem, God Forbid." After that they will read *Snow White and the Seven Dwarves* and live happily ever after.

If you accept the intelligence and the mind that God gave you and the personality that comes with it, with good intention and excellent thought, your life will have an excellent ride on the smooth sea of life. You will be the creator of peace and the peace of heaven will fill your heart within the creation. The creation admires and loves the creator and the creation will assist the creator. Wave after wave of inspiration will flow constantly to the shores of your imagination, dream, hope and expectation. When the imagination, dream, hope and expectation come from a higher source, they will not be foiled. The creation is in flux in every moment and in every instance. It is the living eternal force of the heart of existence, the sustaining power or *Al Kayyum*.

Life is easy and life is difficult. Life is easy if you say so and life is difficult if you say so.

Suppose there are two glasses, one is filled with whiskey and one is filled with orange juice. The one with the whiskey will have the same effect as poison that drives the intelligence away and separates the spirit from the body. But then, many people call the whiskey spirit, so there should not be any difference between the spirit that is in the glass and the spirit that is in the body, because both are spirit. So, spirit should strengthen spirit. This is a notion in the mind of some people that becomes a strong formulation. On the other hand, the least you can say about the orange juice in the other glass, obviously, is that it has no poison. But many will choose the whiskey. Deep within, they know it will bring everything within them to a lower level, but on the spur of the moment, when the spur of the moment comes from the lower desires, they choose the whiskey. The spur of the moment encounters the pure moment which is the moment of consciousness, the moment of peace, tranquility, the moment of nature and the true reality. So, the negative self always operates on the spur of the moment. And the spur of the moment is in supreme command of the human being when the human being is in the forgetful state.

Whenever a human being is in the forgetful state, it is very easy to slip into any situation that is commanded by the lower desires, without even noticing the process that is taking him to the lower state. The spur of the moment always has the upper hand, because it does not require discipline, will power, strength and determination. That is the cause of the state of anxiety, tension, confusion and disasters for millions and millions of people, wherever there are people, whether on earth or Jupiter.

Even if they go to the moon, they will pollute the moon and destroy its magic, romance and the light that fills the night — the moon that inspired dreamers, lovers, poets, artists, Scheherazade, Cleopatra and Marc Antony and cowboys with their ballads around the fire, drinking coffee and whiskey, playing guitar, singing with the moonlight. While they are singing and having a good time, somebody quietly sneaks behind them to the corral and rustles their favorite prized heifer and puts it in a rocket and goes to the moon with it. There he will make of the prized Hereford prized steak and barbecue on an artificial computer fire, because there is no air on the moon.

When the cowboys find out what has happened, they will be extremely upset. They will charge to their horses and ride them without saddles, so as to not waste time and run on the trail of the rocket. Then, when the rocket goes up in the air, they will be running in circles, just like the red Indians when they run in circles around the circle formations of the wagon trains. But the Indian circle around the wagon train will yield some results by the arrows and bullets exchanged, while the circle of the cowboys around the rocket yields nothing except frustration. When they learn their heifer will be slaughtered on the moon, they will look to the moon and it will not be the same. Instead of the moon being a source of joy and romance, it will become a source of sadness and slaughter.

꙰

Intelligence and spirit are powerful forces that stand next to God.

Those Lost Days

When a man feels unhappy, complains, feels bad and cannot relax, he walks around with a sulky, scowling face. He is obsessed with dismal thoughts and his face has a gaunt look, as if calamity is projected in his eyes. He is dispirited with a dreary disposition and his neck gives the impression of calcification. If he is a bigot, abhorrence, and abomination never leave his mind. He is a loathsome lone ranger, roaming from bar to bar in search of his lost identity that might be found in a mate, who is also lost in these dingy bars and who is also searching for her lost identity – and two lost people are better than one – to console, prop and consolidate each other in their predicament and predestination in a life of lost days. In their lost path, they seek a tropical island, but they are really pushing toward the North Pole.

A smooth freeway leads them to the fast lane. The faster they go, the less meaning is left in the life. You might call a highway a freeway, but it is only a freeway to faster tension and creates from a human being a machine that is glued to a wheel, that is glued to a machine, that is glued to four wheels.

And where is this advanced and sophisticated human being going to? I guess he is going to an office or a shop or a factory. And what will he be doing there? If he is in an office, he will be shovelling papers, working on a computer, filing, making photocopies, sending faxes, opening mail, answering the telephone and keeping records of data and events and stacks of papers on papers, in files on files on files, in boxes on boxes on boxes, in file cabinets on file cabinets on file cabinets, in storage room, on storage room, on storage room, year after year after year.

And these papers become extremely important and are guarded vehemently, assiduously, and notoriously, as if they were the treasure of gold, diamonds and precious stone, lapis, jewels, rubies, sapphires, opals, emeralds, and pearls that were found by Ali Baba in Open Sesame.

They have tons upon tons of papers. If they got all these papers and stuck them together in the center of Central Park, they would have a mountain higher than Mt. Everest in the Himalayan Mountains. Then, they could call it the "World's Biggest Monument," to attract tourists. They could plant trees on it and call it the "Modern Hanging Garden." All the artists could carve caves to display their art work, and smoke, drink coffee and meditate on their paintings. They could dress like the people in the Himalayas to give them a different identity as an artist to attract more tourists.

What's going on in all these offices where they shovel papers is the most puzzling phenomenon in the history of humanity since the time of Adam and Eve. Of course, in the time of Adam and Eve, there were no papers except fig leaves that they used as bikinis which were more inclined to fit their environmental simplicity and sophisticated apparel needs of their natural habitat.

Then, there is the office of Mr. Clerk Wiseman, who has been working there for 60 years. The office is in an old building filled with holes and has no windows. And there are tribes of mice who inhabit these caves. Mr. Clerk Wiseman is very attached to them. He works there from 7 o'clock in the morning until 9 o'clock in the evening. Most other workers leave the office by 5 o'clock, but he stays late to continue shovelling papers, because he has become attached to the mice. He and they have developed an affinity to each other. He gathers what is left of crumbs that are left by other workers. He buys Velveeta cheese for the mice. For mice, the taste of Velveeta is equal to the French Camembert cheese that Marie Antoinette used to eat for snacks all day long.

Always at 9 o'clock, he pulls out a tray and fills it with whatever is left over of crumbs, cookies and cheese and puts it on the floor in the middle of the office. He sits next to it eating his dinner. All the mice join him and he talks to them and they sit on his lap and climb on his shoulders. He talks to them and sings to them. This is now a ritual for him to do every night.

While working during the day, he has a pot of coffee next to his desk. Next to the pot, he has all kinds of cakes. In one of the drawers of his desk, he has many assortments of cookies and chocolates, like Lorna Doone, Oreos, Fig Newtons, chocolate chips, Twinkies, Hostess Cupcakes, HoHos, Ding Dongs, Hershey Bars, Milky Ways, Snickers, Three Musketeers, Almond Joy, potato chips with hot dog flavor, steak flavor, barbecue chicken flavor and pork chop flavor.

Mr. Clerk Wiseman has a cup of coffee every hour. He liked to keep all these goodies in his desk so as not to be far away from them. He is very attached to them and calls them divine food. Heaven is in his desk drawer and he will never close that drawer. He has claustrophobia from closing the drawer, because he feels prevented from the heaven. He wants to be very divine and keeps the drawer open to be able to smell and look in the heaven.

One time, one of the girls in the office closes the heaven drawer to permit the space to be open, because the papers are all over the desk, on the wall, under the desk and wherever you look. She thinks that if she closed the drawer, there will be space for leg movement. Meanwhile, Mr. Clerk Wiseman is downstairs at the street corner ordering a pizza with everything on it. He loves anchovies and he loves pepperoni and he loves sausage, green peppers, onion, green and black olives, tomatoes, mushrooms and spinach to balance the pizza to give it the appearance of health food. And he loves pigs' knuckles on the top of that and fried chicken gizzards to top it all off.

When he comes back to his desk and he sees the heaven drawer closed, he goes into convulsions and starts shaking. His eyes become red and he shouts, "I cannot take it. I lost my contact with heaven."

His cheeks are quivering and his eyeballs are going in circles and his head starts to follow the circle movement of his eyes.

All the people at the office are astonished and flabbergasted and they can not figure out why he is moving his head in a circle. One fellow says, "When I was in Afghanistan, I saw a dervish moving his head in circles. And I saw a book on Clerk Wiseman's desk and the title of it was *The Secret Circle Movement of the Head, Its Mystical Implication,* by the renowned Sufi Master John Cagney V, whose great great grandfather, Lord Cagney I, high admiral in Her Majesty's Navy of Queen Victoria, was ordered by the Queen to go find all the secrets of the dervishes in Yemen. Lord Cagney found the dervishes and developed a liking to them. They taught him how to eat glass and chew scorpions. He reported his findings to the Queen.

As for Mr. Clerk Wiseman, because of that event taking place in the office, he has a nervous breakdown. The doctor tells him the first thing he has to do is lose sixty pounds and that this fat is danger fat made of cookies. But the best thing to do is to quit working and leave all those papers to the mice. Go to a little village, go fishing and live happily every after. Know that shovelling that much paper is not a normal action of a human being. It is only when people are demented that they put value in papers.

The situation with shops, stores and factories is that they all produce more than what is needed and then this causes depression. But the real depression is in the brains of the people. If they grow vegetables and eat them, they will cure the depression and the economic crisis.

When people don't use their faculties, intelligence and discernment, they become imbeciles. This kind of imbecility only exists with people who are shallow, who are victims and slaves to their senses and lower desires, and who are lost to themselves, to the beautiful world, to the creation, and to the reality. The existence discards them as a form to a dark, shadowy, sinister reality of liquor, pollution, junk food, weakness, sickness and useless thoughts, which continue until they die. And to exist or not to exist is the same, if the intelligence of the *fitra*, the natural and pure, unpolluted intelligence, which is part of the cycle of the cosmos in the universal plan, is not present. This is an indication of not knowing who you are. Deep within, there are signs of imbecility.

When a man has been given illustrious, prolific intelligence and abundant qualities to lift him to heaven, the real heaven and not the heaven drawer but abuses them and treats them like a child playing with marbles, then he becomes a victim of conflict, problems and confusion. His mind loses its sound functions and his intelligence loses its brilliance and unlimited capacity.

The nature of true intelligence is positive, creative and dynamic. When a man is with the intelligence of the heart, he is with the peace of the moment. But when the man transforms himself from a beautiful human being to an ugly human being, without the understanding of the self, without knowing how to use his positive capacity and higher faculties to bring him to a higher development, to be attuned with the environment and the creation, and without knowing how to bring a balance between the inside of himself and the outside, between the spirit and material, then he is actually punishing himself, as long as he lives this way by his own choice and doing.

Ghazzali said, "Punishment is the natural working out of consequences and not arbitrary inflictions."

God said in the Koran, "We wronged them not, but they wanted to wrong themselves."

"A slave mind," as the Koran says, "plainly is incapable of doing anything good and great."

And Abu Amr Ibn Aala said, "Ignorance abases man and knowledge ennobles him."

The abusive, unnatural and unreal obsession in the glorification of papers is unhealthy to the mind. It causes defects in the intelligence; it makes people morons. The bulk of these papers have no importance and no real function to the people. They are supposed to serve the people, but what is happening is that the people become the servant and the slaves to these papers. The paper has the value and the human being has no value without the paper. It is an inverted state of existence which sinks human beings to the lowest state of the low.

೮ు౮ఇ

John Brown

If a person has no concern for others, this is because he has no concern for himself. When a person has no concern for himself, it means that he is not aware and has no awareness, therefore, he doesn't know how to be concerned with himself or what to do with concern.

John Brown was sitting in a room when Tom came in saying, "Hi, John Brown!" And John Brown said, "Hi, Tom," without enthusiasm or concern. The greeting that took place was action and reaction just like when you hit a tennis ball against the ground and it bounces back to you. So the "hi" that came from Tom bounced back to him from John Brown. And this was the beginning and the end of the conversation, because there was no concern or interest. John Brown's sole interest was to be at peace with himself by drinking beer and eating fried hot dogs soaked in a bowl of mustard mixed with mayonnaise and relish. That was the beginning and the end of everything. And it was the beginning and end of conversation, because there was no concern or interest. And that was the beginning and the end of Tom's evening of chat and progressive thinking.

Tom was educated in London. He admired and was charmed by the code of conduct and ethics of the Victorian Age and he learned how to approach the social circles tactfully. But Tom's approach to John Brown's circle didn't produce anything. His Victorian etiquette didn't bend, not even a bit, the puritanical attitude of John Brown that bound him to fulfill God's wish on earth.

Talk and conversation for John Brown was the loose and sinful way of the unbeliever who smiles all the time. The smile was mockery against God, while a stiff, grim face was respect to God. John Brown said, "I want every moment of my life to be utter respect for God, because I don't want him to be angry at me or he will put me in hell fire. When you work all your life around hot furnaces, where the metal and lead melt, first like chewing gum and then like water, you know about hell fire."

"I once saw a rat fall in the melting lead and it melted and disappeared and was gone. Nothing was left of the rat, not even the skinny tail. I was afraid and I was scared and I was terrified and I was shocked and I was confused and I was shaky. I went quickly to Shaky Pizza, because I thought that the name Shaky might correct my shakiness. And I ate Shaky Pizza and my shake stopped."

"I do not want to melt like the rat in the hell fire. Let me tell you, when the metal and lead melt they start to bubble. If they fall on the ground, they will run like a waterfall on a rocky mountain. If the rat can disappear and melt in a second in the lead, then you will understand what hell fire is like.

"I know what hell fire is like, unlike a person who sits in a cool coffee shop drinking cool cola with ice. In fact, it is the ice in the glass more than the cola by which that person truly causes the wrath of God, by not paying attention to the hereafter life. In the hereafter life, he will be drinking melting lead instead of the cola, with a hot, red charcoal fire for the ice."

John Brown had no idea that a social circle exists or what a social circle is. The only circle that he knew goes around and around in the hot furnace to stir the melting lead at the factory, where the person in charge of the stirring gets an asthma attack.

The only other word he knew that came close to a circle is the "circulation" of a small newspaper, where his brother worked. His brother told him that the circulation of the newspaper was on the rise, because it specialized in the circle news of crime, violation, theft, stealing, killing, embezzlement, corruption, disaster, citations for parking tickets and speeding tickets and all the trade of the so-called age of material and technology that was working very, very hard to bring civilization to the highest zenith of development, harmony, generosity, giving and loving, and to create utopia for humanity.

In Arabic, there is a proverb that says, "Oh God, make things easy and not difficult."

John Brown never had interest in talking with other people, regardless of who they were. All his interest was in his piecework at the factory where he installed hinges on iron doors. He had been doing this for fifty-five years. And he was thinking of working five more years before retiring to give him some extra money. He could use it for more beer and hot dogs.

Also, he would be doing justice to the factory by not quitting so soon, especially when he thought that no one in the world could do his work. He knew that in five more years, when he quit, they would give him a fat bonus. And he loved anything that was fat whether chickens, roosters or fat women because he was so skinny. Actually, you could say that he was like a walking skeleton who ran away from the pyramid because the Pharaoh was after him.

The reason why the Pharaoh was after him was because a fat, soul dancer complained to the Pharaoh that John Brown, the Tourist, had approached her and winked at her and pinched her while she was doing her meditative soul dance, to receive the spirit from the sun. This caused palpitations in her psyche that caused a quivering and vibration in the brain, that caused complex confusion in the descending rays of the sun, that caused shock and rigorous regressing. The spirit of the sun went from being bright and beautiful to dark and ugly.

So, John Brown thought that after five years more he would get a fat bonus for being the longest old-timer in the factory. He spent a solid fifty-five years of work with only one week's vacation in fifty-five years.

Actually, John Brown felt extremely bad and unhappy about having had that one week vacation in fifty-five years for many reasons. First, he said, "I lost money by not working that week."

"Second, I spent money for food at a diner whereas if I had been working, I would have had a sandwich. The sandwich was much more economical, because it was made of two slices of Wonder Bread. This was the best way to eat your fill and save a fortune or a considerable amount of money. The cost of the sandwich was only a few pennies. It was sweet and delicious. The white, gummy bread was like melting chewing gum that sticks to the teeth. You have to lick it with your tongue."

"Someone told me that licking the gooey, sticky, white bread on the teeth will make a man eloquent. In the Middle East they say, 'The beauty of a man is in his eloquence.' So, I am, according to that proverb, eloquently beautiful, because I have been chewing white bread all my life. In fact, I use it as chewing gum to increase the vigor of my jaw."

"Another proverb from the Middle East says, 'A healthy jaw will chew better than a weak jaw.' And jaw breaker candy will be like M&M candy when it feels the grinding of my jaw. That is why it melts in my hand before it finds its way to my mouth."

"The third reason, by not working one week was that I halted the procession and the progress of human civilization for one week. And I felt guilty for it; I felt that taking one day off from work was the biggest sin."

"Mohammed said, 'Work for your life as if you live forever. And work for your later days as if you die tomorrow.' I like that saying. It is like cold cola in the factory at summertime in the middle of August, when the temperature gets to 120 degrees. Next to the iron furnace, it gets to 140 decrees. No one dares come near that spot except me, because I don't believe in being a sinner and running away from the heat around the furnace."

"Fourth, I feel that I have deprived some people by not finishing their iron doors at the proper time. And that has made it easier for thieves to get inside the house to steal a thermos for hot coffee. I feel responsible for the unpleasant, mean, horrible, base, uncivilized, immoral and cruel theft of the thermos for the hot coffee."

"Fifth, I think that, if this happened, I would absolutely not be able to face it or face my calm and tender disposition or the co-workers at the factory."

"Sixth, I have had to go to a psychologist, because I lost sleep at night thinking about all the money I lost by not working one week. But in time, I regained my sleep."

"The best way to combat the thieves is to send them to a concentration camp in the North Pole to protect the citizens. After a while, I reflected on this matter of the thieves and the North Pole and I changed my mind, because if there were no thieves, no one would buy the iron doors. That means I would loose my job. And I am planning to work five more years. So, it was better not to tell anyone about my idea for at least five years. Besides, the thieves are only poor people who need to drink hot coffee. The more they drink hot coffee, the more there will be a need for iron doors."

"God has a reason for making some people thieves. So, who am I to judge God's wisdom. I am here only to please God. I say 'Hooray' for the thieves of the thermos of hot coffee. May God bless and invigorate them and make the winter very, very cold and the summer, cold. Then, the thieves will drink more coffee. That means they will have to steal more thermoses. That means selling more iron doors and that will mean more money for me. And, in five years, I will retire and go to Key West to live in a condominium, with a small swimming pool, because I can't swim in the ocean. My skin is sensitive to salt. I can't look at the sun, because of working in a dark factory all my life. The hot iron furnace caused my eyes to twitch permanently. The twitch gets more quivering when I am in the sun."

"Also, I can't breathe pure air because in the factory I breathe carbon monoxide. My nose starts to shake and sniff like a rabbit, but my sniffing is for a whiff of air, while the rabbit is sniffing because he smells organic carrot juice. Somebody left it in a bowl and has gone to buy a cola, because he likes to mix cola and organic carrot juice."

Also, I have an allergy to sea gulls, even if they are ten miles away. I can't breathe and my eyes get crimson red and my heart starts to shake and I loose control of my speech. I start to gibber and talk in tongues and my blood gets mixed with all the chemical's fumes."

৪ও৩

Other Books by Adnan Sarhan:
Wake Up or Sleep Forever
Spirit and Technology
When Life is Lovable and Love is Livable
The Enchanted Oasis of the Ringed Dove
The Final Abode of Consumer Society
Dance Your Way to Spirit